For Mom, Dad, Samantha, and Nate.
Thanks for always supporting me and my dreams.

URBAN
MEYER

★ ★ ★ ★ ★ ★ ★ VS. ★ ★ ★ ★ ★ ★ ★

COLLEGE
FOOTBALL

THE CASE FOR **COLLEGE FOOTBALL'S GREATEST COACH**

BEN AXELROD

TRIUMPH
BOOKS

No part of this publication may be reproduced, stored in a retrieval system, or transmitted in any form by any means, electronic, mechanical, photocopying, or otherwise, without the prior written permission of the publisher, Triumph Books LLC, 814 North Franklin Street, Chicago, Illinois 60610.

Library of Congress Cataloging-in-Publication Data available upon request

This book is available in quantity at special discounts for your group or organization. For further information, contact:

Triumph Books LLC
814 North Franklin Street
Chicago, Illinois 60610
(312) 337-0747
www.triumphbooks.com

Printed in U.S.A.
ISBN: 978-1-62937-463-5
Design by Patricia Frey
Photos courtesy of AP Images unless otherwise indicated

Contents

★ ★ ★
Acknowledgments

This book was written over the course of many self-manufactured long weekends at the Grandview Heights Public Library in the winter of 2017 and powered by several Starbucks Venti—and sometimes Trenta—cold brew coffees.

It wouldn't have been possible if not for the support from the leadership group at Cox Media Group and LandOf10.com, including James de Gale, Michael Carvell, and Michael Bass. I also want to thank my Ohio State cohorts at Land of 10, Jeremy Birmingham and Ryan Ginn, for trusting me while taking on such a daunting project.

A special thanks to Urban Meyer and the Ohio State football program, specifically the communications department led by Jerry Emig and Adam Widman, and the many players I have covered over the course of my career.

I would also like to acknowledge those who covered Urban Meyer at Bowling Green, Utah, and Florida, and the many members of the Ohio State beat, past and present, whose hard work helped contribute to this book, as well as some whose friendship has always made the busiest time of the year more enjoyable than it should be. Thank you Ari Wasserman, Austin Ward, David Briggs, Kyle Rowland, Tim Shoemaker, Bill Landis,

Tim May, Eric Seger, and Tony Gerdeman, among others. Thanks to my friend and mentor, Zac Jackson.

Thank you to my former employers: Bleacher Report, Frank Moskowitz at Buckeye Sports Bulletin, Kevin Noon at Buckeye Grove, John Porentas at The Ozone, and Dan Caterinicchia at Ohio State.

Thank you to Tim, Scott, Michael S., Michael W., and Andrew.

Last but not least, thank you, Torey. I couldn't have written this book without your love and encouragement.

★ ★ ★
Introduction

Urban Meyer stood in the northeast corner of Arlington, Texas' AT&T Stadium, confetti raining from the sky as his players belted out their rendition of Ohio State's alma mater, "Carmen, Ohio" for the final time of the 2014 season.

The Buckeyes' head coach clutched his daughter Gigi and son, Nate, and soon his other daughter, Nicki, and wife, Shelley, joined the semi-circle embrace. Tears made a cameo in the eyes of each of the five Meyers.

No matter what had happened before, or what would after, this was the culmination of a run that would define Urban Meyer's career and forever etch his name next to the giants of his industry. It was the greatest coaching job in college football history.

Moments earlier, Ohio State had sealed a 42–20 victory over Oregon to win the inaugural College Football Playoff championship. This, however, was the rare instance in which another national title appeared to merely be a cherry on top. Truth be told, Meyer had already staked his claim to overcoming college football's most difficult obstacles a game earlier—if not two.

It's one thing to win a third national championship and it's another to do it in a foreign postseason format. But to beat three of college football's top teams while down to your third-string quarterback? That will forever put a head coach in rarefied air.

And yet that's exactly the predicament Meyer found himself facing as starting quarterback J.T. Barrett was carted off the field in the Buckeyes' 2014 regular season finale against Michigan. Ohio State had already clinched a spot in the Big Ten Championship Game and all but secured an 11–1 regular season record. A win over Wisconsin for the conference title would likely solidify the Buckeyes' case to make the first-ever College Football Playoff.

It seemed improbable at the time, considering Ohio State entered Indianapolis as a four-point underdog against the Badgers. With star quarterback Braxton Miller lost to injury two weeks before the season and now Barrett dealing with a broken ankle, Meyer was down to a lightly recruited, seldom-used, third-string quarterback named Cardale Jones. Even if the Buckeyes could find a way to pick up a win over Wisconsin, anything they accomplished after would be considered gravy.

Yet not only would Ohio State beat the Badgers 59–0—behind an MVP performance from Jones—but as the No. 4 seed in the first-ever playoff, Ohio State toppled the nation's top-ranked team, Alabama, in the semifinal Sugar Bowl. What would follow would be a one-sided demolition of the Ducks in the national title game, capping one of the most unlikely and historic championship runs in college football history.

"Very humbled. I've got my third-string quarterback sitting here to my left. I've never met a third-string quarterback before, and he's 3–0," Meyer said after the game. "We're officially brothers for the rest of our lives because we're champions."

It's a feeling Meyer is plenty familiar with.

With Ohio State's win over Oregon at the end of the 2014 season, the then-13th-year head coach won his third national title and joined Nick Saban as just the second coach to win national championships at multiple programs. With a career 154–27 record to his credit and two undefeated seasons on top of his three national title campaigns, there's no doubting the numbers when it comes to Meyer's coaching career. He's unquestionably one of the best to ever do it in the sport.

But is he *the* best? On the surface, it may seem like a tough case to make.

Some coaches have more rings and others have more wins than Meyer. And let's just get to the elephant in the room: with the way Nick Saban's Alabama program is currently hitting on all cylinders, it'd be tough to argue that any other coach—let alone one of Saban's contemporaries and rivals—has a more legitimate claim to being considered the greatest college football coach of all time.

But while Meyer's résumé—although still impressive—may fall short numerically, his legacy is hardly one that can purely be measured by numbers.

Few coaches have built—and sustained—success as frequently as Meyer has during stints at Bowling Green, Utah, Florida, and Ohio State. Even fewer coaches can claim to have cracked college football's recruiting code or to have found the key to turning historic rivalries into one-sided affairs.

Need proof of Meyer's game-planning acumen? Take a look at his record coming off bye weeks or in bowl games. Looking for evidence of his player development? Look no further than the plethora of players he's put into the pros—at all different positions.

More than anything, Meyer's rise up the college football coaching ranks has been unlike any other in the history of the sport. From nameless position coach to hotshot headman to national champion to early retirement and a rebirth many never saw coming, Meyer's journey to his place in the coaching pantheon has been one of a kind—just like his run to his third national title.

What follows is a case for Meyer's status as the greatest coach in college football history, how he got there, and how he compares with his rivals, idols, and other coaching greats. By design, Meyer wasn't involved in the process of writing this book. In fact, I'd imagine he hates the idea of having his legacy stacked up against those of other coaching legends. If there's one thing the Ohio State head coach has learned how to do in the last five years, it's to live in the moment.

The historical-perspective stuff, or "noise," as he would term it? That's for writers like me.

I don't have a Mount Rushmore and I don't have a personal top 10 when it comes to college football coaches. Quite frankly, I'm not even too keen on the idea of comparing coaching résumés. Each coach's trajectory includes its own special set of circumstances.

What I do have is an understanding of the uniqueness of Meyer's career and its place in college football history. Just like a third-string quarterback winning a national championship, it's something we may never see again.

But before stacking up where Meyer's coaching legacy stands, let's first take a look at how he got here.

PART I

★ ★ ★

The Making of Urban Meyer

★ ★ ★

A Kid from Ashtabula

Urban Frank Meyer III was born July 10, 1964, in Toldeo, Ohio, to Gisela and Bud Meyer. Bud was a chemical engineer and Gisela was a gourmet cook who had escaped Nazi Germany as a young girl.

When Urban was five years old, his family moved to Ashtabula, a small town on Ohio's northeast border.

"I'm a big fan [of Ashtabula]," Meyer said following his annual youth camp in Geneva, Ohio, just outside of Ashtabula, in 2016. "Everyone knows that. I'm very proud of where I came from.

"I had it really good. I had a great group of coaches, great teachers, great high school. Great friends here that I'm still very close with; I just wish I could come back more."

Urban was a middle child, sandwiched between two sisters. All three of the Meyer children were athletes. In Bud's house, you didn't have a choice.

"Everybody had to do sports," Bud said in Buddy Martin's 2008 biography of Urban, *Urban's Way*.

"I don't know how you didn't do sports. We're one of those families, tragically, that has absolutely no artistic ability whatsoever. We can't even write a decent poem. None of us plays a musical instrument. I'm not proud of it. But everybody has to do something sports-wise just because that's how you're supposed to do it. I don't know things differently."

Urban's older sister Gigi was a member of the Saint John High School swim team, and Erica played golf and softball. Urban, meanwhile, shined on the gridiron and baseball diamond.

While Urban was a natural athlete, his father made sure his son developed a work ethic. Whenever Urban would strike out looking, Bud famously made his son run home from the game.

On the football field, Meyer starred as both the starting tailback and free safety for the Fighting Heralds. He wore jersey No. 45 in honor of his favor player, Ohio State running back Archie Griffin. Among his friends and teammates growing up was Dean Hood, who would go on to serve as the defensive coordinator at Wake Forest and head coach at Eastern Kentucky.

Rushing for more than 800 yards and defending nine passes, Meyer was named first-team All–Ohio Northern and all-state in his senior season in 1981.

But while football was his first love, baseball was Meyer's best sport.

"He was like a stud when he came in for his junior year," Saint John head coach Bill Schmidt told BuckeyeSports.com in 2011. "Then things started to take off for him. His forte was he had a cannon for an arm, and playing shortstop, that's what you need. He was able to make all the plays, and I would say his signature play was when he would go deep in the hole at short, round it off and make that throw over."

Following a senior season in which the 6'2", 180-pound shortstop showcased a .370 batting average, the Atlanta Braves opted to select Meyer in the 13th round of the 1982 MLB draft. He was picked ahead of future baseball stars Jose Canseco, Bret Saberhagen, and Kenny Rogers.

What followed, however, was an unmemorable two-year stint in Atlanta's minor league system. All of 17 years old, Meyer hit for an unimpressive .170 in his first 20 games with the Gulf Coast League Braves. In 1983, he began with Pulaski in the Appalachian League, before being recalled to the GCL after 15 games.

Meyer's two-season stat line in the Braves' system was meager: 44 games, 20 hits in 138 at-bats and a .182 batting average. A case of tendinitis in his throwing arm brought Meyer's minor league baseball career to an unmemorable end. When he finally received his release papers from the Braves, they were signed by the organization's then-director of player development, Hank Aaron.

"I just wasn't good enough," Meyer told the Atlanta *Journal-Constitution*'s Michael Carvell in 2014. "I was a really good high school football player. I was doing OK my second year [with the Braves], and then I had an injury to my arm. But I had already probably maximized my ability."

Along the way, Meyer played alongside future major leaguers Fred McGriff, Mark Lemke, and Ron Gant. But although he was unable to join them in the "big show," a part of Meyer's success today is rooted in his failures from more than 25 years ago.

After his first disappointing season in the GCL, Meyer wanted to quit. So much so that he called Bud to inform him of his plans.

Bud, however, had other ideas. He could no longer force his son to run home from practice, but according to *Urban's Way*, the message Meyer received from his father was quite clear.

"OK, you're seventeen and you're grown. So you're capable of making your own decision. But by the way, you're not welcome back here," Bud told Urban, per the biography. "I'm sure your mother would want to see you at Christmas, but other than that, you're not welcome. There are no quitters in the Meyer family."

With that, Meyer stuck with it, continuing his baseball career until he was literally no longer able to, physically. In many ways, that helped forge the work ethic Meyer is best known for today, whether it be the furthering of his success or making corrections after a rare loss.

"It didn't hurt him," Bud Meyer told the *New York Times* in 2007. "It gave him a lot of maturity."

When it came to college football, perhaps it shouldn't come as a surprise that Bud Meyer revered hard-nosed coaches like Ohio State's Woody Hayes and Michigan's Bo Schembechler, while Gisela was a Notre Dame fan.

Gisela saw her son serve as an assistant coach for her favorite team before passing away in 2000 following a fight with cancer. After a battle with lung disease, Bud died on November 10, 2011—17 days before Urban was announced as Ohio State's head coach.

His memory, however, has lived on within his son's teams. With each freshman class he brings in, Meyer tells his new players the story of how his father refused to allow him to leave the Braves after his first year.

Perhaps it shouldn't come as a surprise that Meyer has shaped his programs in the same way the most influential figure in his life has shaped him.

★ ★ ★

Getting Back to the Gridiron

With his baseball career having come to an unceremonious end, Meyer did what most 19-year-olds whose dreams had been dashed would do: he went home.

But after a brief stint as an assistant baseball coach at Cleveland State University, Meyer plotted a return to his first love—and in the process, out of Northeast Ohio.

At 20, he enrolled at the University of Cincinnati, which had become somewhat of a pipeline program for the Meyer family. Urban's grandfather taught traffic law at UC and Bud had graduated from the school's

College of Engineering in 1957. A year before Urban arrived, his older sister, Gigi, graduated with an undergraduate degree and would later work as a vice provost for undergraduate affairs.

Meyer's ceiling on the gridiron wasn't as high as it had been on the baseball diamond, but nevertheless, he plotted a return to the football field. Joining head coach Dave Currey's Bearcats program as a walk-on, Meyer returned to his former position of safety—although his playing time was admittedly limited.

As Cincinnati endured a grueling 2–9 campaign, Meyer tallied two tackles, both of which came in a 48–17 loss to Florida. According to the Bearcats' media guide, he also spent time as a holder on field goals and point-after attempts.

"I probably wasn't a good enough player to go there," Meyer admitted in 2014, a week before his Buckeyes faced off with his alma mater. "It wasn't a great experience. We weren't very good."

Perhaps soured by the taste of losing and spotty playing time, Meyer left the Cincinnati program, although he remained an active member of the Sigma Chi fraternity. At a Derby Days party with the Zeta Tau Alpha sorority in May 1984, he met a fair queen from Ohio's Ross County named Shelley Mather. The two would later date and wed in 1989.

Although his playing career had come to an end, Meyer's coaching career was just getting started. In 1985, he served as a volunteer assistant at Cincinnati prep powerhouse St. Xavier, coaching the defensive backs.

Even more than 30 years ago, Meyer showed signs of becoming the same coach who now intensely stalks the Ohio Stadium sidelines on Saturdays in the fall.

"He was in your face both ways—if you did something right or something wrong," former St. Xavier running back and defensive back Steve Specht told MaxPreps.com in 2012. "I think true football players gravitate toward that. Kids feed off of it."

Upon graduating from UC, Currey offered Meyer a job as a graduate assistant with the Bearcats, which he nearly accepted. Only a better offer had come just over 100 miles north from Ohio State head coach Earl Bruce.

"I had some opportunities to be a grad assistant at some other schools, but I always wanted to be a Buckeye," Meyer said in an interview with 610 WTVN in 2016. "I wanted to play [at Ohio State] but unfortunately I didn't have enough 'quick twitch' to."

Under Bruce, Meyer served as a grad assistant, working with the Buckeyes tight ends and wide receivers. In his first season in Columbus, he helped oversee the development of one of the all-time greats in Ohio State history in future Pro Football Hall of Fame selection Cris Carter, who caught 69 passes for 1,127 yards and 11 touchdowns as a junior in 1986.

"Urban and I are very good friends. Urban, his first job was coaching wide receivers at Ohio State. He was 22 or 23 at the time, and I had happened to be there," Carter told Fox Sports' Colin Cowherd on his nationally syndicated radio show in 2017. "So he coached me at Ohio State as the wide receivers coach, his first job from the University of Cincinnati as a defensive back, he was hired by Earle Bruce to be the wide receivers coach as a graduate assistant. And that was the year I made first-team All-American. So him and I have been best buddies for a long, long, long time."

Enjoying a 10–3 season, including a first-place finish in Big Ten play, Meyer's Ohio State coaching career was off to a strong start. Unfortunately for the Buckeyes, however, it wouldn't last long.

Much like his junior season, Carter's presence also loomed large over the Ohio State program in 1987—albeit for all the wrong reasons. Just longer than a month before the start of what was supposed to be his senior season, the NCAA ruled Carter ineligible due to his accepting money and signing with an agent.

With that, the Buckeyes went from national title contenders to enduring a 6–4–1 campaign. Six days before they were set to face Michigan in their regular season finale, Bruce was fired, effective following a rivalry game the Buckeyes would go on to win 23–20.

"I can tell you everything," Meyer recalled in 2012. "I can [remember] walking into Coach Bruce's office right here, [the Woody Hayes Athletic Center just opened], and [former OSU athletic director] Rick Bay was leaned up against the wall and looked at me and said, 'Close the door. Are you the last one?' I said, 'Yes, yes, sir.' And I sat down.

"I saw a bunch of coaches with their arms on the table, with their face in their arms, and tears and the whole deal. I was like the last guy to walk in, and [Bay] said that Coach Bruce will no longer be the coach after this game, and I have resigned as athletic director. Like it was right there, right out that door. I have great respect—I knew Mr. Bay very well and have great respect for him. Just an incredible moment in Ohio State history."

Just like that, Meyer was introduced to the realities of big-boy college football, fired by the program he grew up rooting for. Barely even a man, he set forth on a climb up the coaching ranks, catching on as an outside linebackers coach with Jim Heacock's staff at Division I-AA Illinois State.

After two seasons in Normal, Illinois, Meyer rejoined Bruce at Colorado State, where his mentor had become the Rams' head coach. Meyer spent three seasons coaching for Bruce and stayed on for another three years with the Rams after Bruce was fired and replaced with Miami (Florida) defensive coordinator Sonny Lubick.

In Meyer's six seasons in Fort Collins, Colorado State accumulated a 40–31 record. As the wide receivers coach, he oversaw the development of Greg Primus, who left CSU as the school's all-time leader in both receptions (194) and receiving yards (3,263).

As was the case throughout the previous stops of his coaching career, Meyer's trademark intensity was on full display.

"Okay, you take [his intensity] and multiply it by 100, just younger," said Tony Alford, a former Colorado State running back who Meyer hired as his running backs coach at Ohio State in 2015. "He was great. He coached the receivers, but he had some great mentors in Earle. You could tell the guy had a passion and a fire about doing things. Not just doing them, but doing them right and very particular about the finer details of everything that happens."

Meyer's success at Colorado State—both on the field and on the recruiting trail—caught the attention of Notre Dame head coach Lou Holtz, who hired him to coach the Fighting Irish wide receivers in 1996.

For the Catholic boy from Ohio who was named after a succession of popes, the chance to coach under the watch of Touchdown Jesus was a dream come true.

"I still remember the day that I was hired and I took a tour," Meyer said in 2015. "It was very cold, but I took a tour throughout the Touchdown Jesus, Fair Catch Corby, all the great statues and all the great traditions on that campus.

"There are two places that were near and dear to my heart in my entire life, and that was Ohio State and Notre Dame."

Despite coaching the receivers on a team that utilized the option offense, Meyer thrived under Holtz and his successor in South Bend, Bob Davie. In five seasons at Notre Dame, Meyer helped develop Malcolm Johnson into a fifth-round pick of the Pittsburgh Steelers and David Givens into an eventual seventh-round selection for the New England Patriots. In 1999, his receiving corps broke the Fighting Irish single-season record for pass receptions with 192 and total receiving yards with 2,858.

Meyer also began working on a personal basis with a Fighting Irish graduate assistant named Dan Mullen, with the two planting the early seeds of what would eventually become the spread offense. With Notre Dame compiling a 38–22 record over the course of five seasons, Meyer's coaching career appeared to be on an upward trajectory.

His first opportunity as a head coach, however, would arrive far earlier than even he anticipated it would.

Climbing the Coaching Mountain

Nearly a decade prior to the birth of #MACtion, the social media slogan that has helped popularize the unpredictable nature of Mid-American Conference football, Bowling Green State University was in a rut. Under the direction of head coach Gary Blackney, the Falcons had endured six consecutive losing seasons from 1995 to 2000.

Thus, it came of little surprise when Blackney didn't return to BGSU following a 2–9 season at the turn of the new millennium. What was less predictable, however, was that when searching for Blackney's replacement, Falcons athletic director Paul Krebs reached out to a position coach at Notre Dame who couldn't even claim so much as a season as a coordinator to his credit.

"I was asked to interview at Bowling Green by Earle Bruce, who pushed my name very hard; so did Coach Holtz," Meyer recalled during a speech at the annual Lou Holtz/Upper Ohio Valley Hall of Fame banquet in 2013. "I go to interview for the position, not really thinking I want to go to Bowling Green."

Meyer was under the impression that the feeling was mutual.

"I go to interview for the position not thinking I'm going to get it," he said. "I get the phone call, 'We're going to offer you the job.' So I start thinking about it. I loved Notre Dame. My son was born there, he was baptized in the chapel, and I thought, 'Now's not the time. I'm not going to take it.'"

After a conversation with Bruce, which, per Meyer, included some colorful language from the former Ohio State head coach, Meyer turned his attention toward Holtz, his first boss with the Fighting Irish, who had since become a mentor. What followed was a conversation that put into perspective where Meyer stood on the college football coach totem pole.

"Coach, I got offered the job, but I'm not going to take it," Meyer recalled telling Holtz.

"What?" Holtz responded.

"I'm not going to take it," Meyer reiterated.

"Why not?" Holtz inquired.

"I don't believe it's a good job," Meyer relented.

"Of course not," Holtz replied. "If it was a good job, you think they'd be calling you?"

On December 4, 2000, Bowling Green officially introduced Urban Meyer as its 15th head coach in program history.

Taking over a Falcons team coming off a 2–9 campaign, the 36-year-old Meyer had his work cut out for himself. Recruiting had predictably fallen off, and the BGSU facilities didn't offer much to showcase. More urgently, he had inherited a roster full of players who had barely ever heard of their new head coach.

It didn't take them long to find out what Meyer was all about.

Urban Meyer took his first head coaching job at Bowling Green in 2001. He left with a 17–6 overall record.

In his first offseason at Bowling Green, 21 players opted to leave the Falcons program, unable to handle Meyer's stringent demands—both on the field and in the classroom—and his intense off-season workouts.

Fifteen years later, Meyer still remembers the first moment his program was in need of a drastic culture change.

"I walk in the first workout, [the players] are in Budweiser T-shirts, stuff like that," Meyer recalled a week before the Buckeyes faced the Falcons in the first week of the 2016 season. "So we had to—obviously that's not going to make it real well with us."

So Meyer went to the school's outfitter, Adidas, and implored it to supply some gear. More focused on its more premier programs, Adidas allowed the Falcons a stipend of $2,500—enough to buy the team new shirts and a pair of shoes.

"They were blue and gray," Meyer said of the shoes. "[Bowling Green's] colors are orange and brown. But it didn't matter. Man, the kids got blue and gray shoes to wear. That tells you the expectation level of those young people. 'Hey, thanks for the T-shirt, Coach, I appreciate it.' But no one said these aren't our colors. But they got a free T-shirt and a pair of shoes.

"So that was probably the moral of the story or the point of the story is zero expectation. They wanted nothing other than to find somehow to finish their careers with a winning record. That was our whole mantra; finish their career with a winning record, the seniors."

The first game of the Meyer era at Bowling Green would coincide with one of the toughest tests of the Falcons' season.

In Missouri, Bowling Green found itself battling a Big 12 opponent on the road without so much as a full roster to aid the Falcons' efforts.

"I think 50 some players made the travel team," Meyer recalled. "We were allowed to take 70. We didn't have 70 players."

The night before his first game as a head coach, panic crept in as Meyer lay awake in his Columbia, Missouri, hotel room.

"I looked at Shelley [and said], 'What if we lose every game we play?' Because who knew?" Meyer remembers. "She said, 'I bet you win tomorrow.' I looked at her and I said, 'We have no freaking chance of winning this game tomorrow.'"

As it turned out, Shelley was right.

Behind 107 rushing yards from running back Joe Alls, who scored the game-winning touchdown with 3:40 left on the clock, Bowling Green topped the Tigers 20–13 in Meyer's head coaching debut. With a receiving corps Meyer had little faith in when it came to catching the ball, the Falcons were able to confuse Missouri with the early version of their head coach's power spread offense, which featured Andy Sahm and Josh Harris splitting reps at quarterback.

Bowling Green's season-opening upset was just a sign of good things to come for the Falcons, who opened the year on a three-game winning streak and carried a 6–3 record into the second-to-last game of the season. It was then that BGSU faced its second opponent from a major conference, the Big Ten's Northwestern, with the Falcons' flair for the dramatic once again making an appearance.

Falling behind 28–14 to the Wildcats midway through the third quarter, Bowling Green appeared to be headed for its fourth loss of Meyer's debut campaign. An eight-yard touchdown rush from Harris, who was making his second start as the Falcons quarterback, would cut Northwestern's lead to just a touchdown, but the Wildcats responded on the ensuing drive with an 80-yard touchdown pass from Zak Kustok to Kunle Patrick.

Bowling Green, however, wasn't done just yet, answering back on the very next drive with an 18-yard touchdown pass from Harris to receiver

Robert Redd—only to have Northwestern running back Torri Stuckey negate the score with a 12-play, 64-yard touchdown drive.

The Falcons offense would once again issue a response, this time in the form of a Harris three-yard touchdown rush. His defense unable to stop Northwestern's offense, Meyer opted to send the ensuing kickoff short, knowing his team may need the ball back sooner rather than later, as it trailed 42–35 with 2:50 left on the clock.

This time, however, Bowling Green's defense held its own, forcing and recovering a Stuckey fumble and giving Harris the ball back at his own 23-yard line with 1:23 left on the clock. The running back-turned-quarterback proceeded to drive the ball the length of the field, finding Redd for a five-yard touchdown with 36 seconds remaining on the clock. An extra point would tie the game, but Meyer knew he didn't have the horses to keep up in a potential overtime period. Instead, he opted to go for the two-point conversion, with Harris pitching the ball to receiver Cole Magner on a reverse for what would prove to be the game-winning play. Bowling Green 43, Northwestern 42.

"Coaches are weird ducks, man," Meyer said in 2013. "I don't know my address, but I can tell you every play in that game."

It would prove to be the signature victory of Meyer's Falcons tenure.

"We had a six-hour bus ride and we refused to leave the locker room for about two and a half hours," Meyer recalled. "Those kids wouldn't leave and I wouldn't leave with them. We were just crying and enjoying it. It was an incredible comeback."

With a 56–21 victory over rival Toledo a week later, Bowling Green would finish the season with an 8–3 record—making the Falcons the most-improved team in the country following their first winning season in seven years. With Harris transforming into an emerging star, Bowling Green would enter 2002 as a preseason favorite in the MAC West, expectations accompanying Meyer's early success.

And for the first eight weeks of the season, the Falcons lived up to the hype. Compiling an 8–0 record, including a victory in its rematch against Missouri and a win at Kansas, Bowling Green looked like a legitimate BCS buster as the final third of the regular season approached, ranking as high as No. 20 in the Associated Press Top 25.

In the process, Harris became a legitimate dark-horse Heisman Trophy candidate, compiling 3,162 yards of total offense and 39 touchdowns—plus three receptions for 51 yards and two more scores—while directing Meyer's spread attack.

However, Harris' Heisman hopes—and the No. 20–ranked Falcons' postseason dreams—hit a snag in mid-November, as Bowling Green suffered its first loss of the season with a 26–17 defeat at the hands of Northern Illinois. The Falcons would wind up losing three of their final four games, including a season-closing 42–24 loss to Toledo in the Battle of I-75.

It may have been a sour note to close the season on, but in two years, Meyer had amassed an impressive 17–6 record at a program that hadn't enjoyed a winning record since 1994. That was enough to keep Meyer's name as one of the hottest in the coaching market, with Utah hiring him as its new head coach at the end of 2002 season.

"Urban is one of the brightest stars in the coaching fraternity, and he has left our program in tremendous shape," Krebs said following Meyer's departure.

In Salt Lake City, Meyer found himself in charge of a program with firmer footing than the one he had previously taken over. Utah had fired head coach Ron McBride following a 5–6 season in 2002, but the Utes had enjoyed winning seasons in all but two of the previous 10 years.

But while Meyer had more to work with in Utah than he had in Bowling Green, he also stumbled upon his star player with the Utes by accident.

After incumbent starting quarterback Brett Elliott broke his wrist in Utah's second game of the season in 2003 against California, Meyer had no choice but to turn to a seldom-used sophomore with just 11 career pass attempts to his credit.

"A skinny kid came jogging in. I can't remember his name," Meyer said sarcastically in 2014. "Alex Smith or something like that? He did pretty good."

That would be an obvious understatement.

The skinny sophomore from La Mesa, California, would prove to be a nearly perfect fit in Meyer's spread offense, totaling 2,699 yards of total offense (2,247 passing, 452 rushing), 20 total touchdowns and just three interceptions as the Utes captured an outright Mountain West Conference championship with a 10–2 record. Utah's early success under Meyer, however, wasn't simple. In his third season as a head coach, he maintained a habit of living on the edge.

Such was the case in an early-November game at Air Force, which saw the 6–2 Utes give up a 23–7 third-quarter lead, a week after suffering their first conference loss of the season to New Mexico.

With the game lasting until a third overtime, Utah found itself—and its conference championship hopes—on the ropes, trailing 43–37 and in need of a touchdown to keep the game alive. Smith found receiver Steve Savoy for a 22-yard completion on third down to set up a fourth-and-1. From there, a converted tight end–turned–running back named Ben Moa punched in the game-tying score, before winning the game a play later on a pop pass from Moa to tight end Matt Hansen on the difference-making two-point conversion.

Just as he had at Bowling Green, Meyer showed a knack for getting the most out of his players—even while they were playing positions you wouldn't necessarily expect them to.

"Our tailback was hurt," Meyer recalled of the game nine years later. "Alex Smith was our quarterback. He wasn't a great runner, so we put the tight end at quarterback and just kept pounding people.

"One day in practice I said, 'Try this,' he continued, referring to the pop pass. "The first one he almost hit me, and I was nowhere near the receiver. It looked like a tight end throwing the ball, but he got better and better, and we used it and won the game."

In Meyer's second season in Salt Lake City, there was little need for trickeration.

Starting the year as the nation's No. 19–ranked team, the Utes got off to a hot start, climbing to the top 10 of the AP Top 25 by mid-October. As Smith blossomed into one of the nation's top players, the Utes emerged as one of the country's best teams, winning a second straight Mountain West title with an undefeated run through the regular season. Utah's closest contest of the season came in a 49–35 victory over Air Force in late September and its average point differential of plus-25.8 ranked second in the country, trailing only Louisville.

With 3,583 yards of total offense (2,952 passing, 631 rushing) and 42 total touchdowns to his credit, Smith earned an invitation to New York City as a finalist for the Heisman Trophy, finishing No. 4 behind USC quarterback Matt Leinart, Oklahoma running back Adrian Peterson, and Oklahoma quarterback Jason White.

Ranked sixth in the country, Utah was selected for a spot in the 2005 Fiesta Bowl, a BCS bowl game in which the Utes would face their first ranked opponent of the season in No. 20 Pittsburgh. Any questions about Utah's undefeated record being the result of a soft schedule, however, would soon be put to rest. Behind 328 passing yards and four passing scores from Smith, and a Fiesta Bowl–record 15 catches for 198 yards and two touchdowns from wideout Paris Warren, the Utes put an exclamation point on their 12–0 campaign with a 35–7 pummeling of the Panthers.

That off-season, Smith would declare for the NFL draft, where he was selected by the San Francisco 49ers with the first overall pick.

Meyer, too, would be moving on. Prior to co-coaching the Utes in the Fiesta Bowl alongside Utah defensive coordinator Kyle Whittingham, Meyer had accepted an offer to become the head coach of one of the nation's premier programs, Florida.

Prepared to move for a third time in four years, Meyer's oldest daughter, then-14-year-old Nicki, asked about her father's journey.

"Your dad is climbing a mountain," Shelley Meyer explained, per the South Florida *Sun Sentinel*. "That's why we keep moving."

"So is Dad at the top of the mountain yet?" Nicki replied.

"Yes," Shelley answered. "We're going to Florida. That's the top of the mountain."

★ ★ ★

The Florida Years

Meyer's choice to go to Gainesville wasn't as simple as Shelley made it seem.

Having compiled a 39–8 record, including two conference championships and an undefeated season in a four-year span, and having just turned 40 years old, Meyer had emerged as the hottest head coach in all of college football. As Utah's undefeated 2004 campaign came to a close, it was only a matter of time before he wound up at a major program.

Among the openings in college football were not just Florida, but also LSU and Notre Dame. Pretty soon it became clear that his choice was ultimately going to be between a Gators program looking for a bump back into college football's elite and the already-familiar Fighting Irish.

In the days leading into Utah's Fiesta Bowl selection, a semipublic tug-of-war between Florida and Notre Dame broke out. Per the *Sun Sentinel*'s Jeff Darlington, Meyer spurned what he had once deemed his "dream job" in South Bend for the opportunity to build something of his own with the Gators.

"If you want a good coaching job, you should go to Florida," Bud Meyer told his son, per Darlington. "But if you want to be someone immortal with a bronze statue, I don't think that comes with Florida."

Urban reportedly responded, "I just want to coach. I don't want to write books. I don't want to give speeches for $30,000 a pop. I just want to coach."

Earle Bruce agreed; Meyer should go to the Gators. With that the boy from Ashtabula, Ohio, accepted a reported seven-year, $14 million contract to become Florida's 22nd head football coach.

For four years, Meyer had largely beaten opponents based on his ability to outscheme them while putting his players in the best positions to succeed. Now he'd have the talent that comes along with a top-level program and one of the most fertile recruiting territories in all of college football.

In three seasons under the direction of Meyer's predecessor, the Gators had recruited well, but failed to keep up on the field with in-state rivals Miami and Florida State. In three seasons as the successor to Florida legend Steve Spurrier, Ron Zook had amassed a 23–14 record, never winning more than eight games in a single season.

In hiring Meyer—and firing Zook—the expectations of Gators athletic director Jeremy Foley were clear: return Florida to national prominence, where it was when it won a national title under Spurrier in 1996.

Meyer, however, wasn't starting from scratch. In his three seasons in Gainesville, Zook had recruited three top-10 classes, including two top-five hauls and the nation's No. 1 class in 2003. And while he may not have been a perfect fit for his new head coach's spread offense, Meyer inherited both an experienced and a talented starting quarterback in former five-star prospect Chris Leak.

Starting Meyer's first season ranked No. 10 in the country, a 4–0 start to the year catapulted Florida to as high as No. 5 in the AP Top 25. In their fifth game, however, the Gators lost to No. 15 Alabama two weeks before suffering another defeat at the hands of No. 10 LSU. Florida dropped to No. 16 nationally before winning three of its final four regular season games to finish No. 2 in the SEC East.

In one season under Meyer, Florida had improved its record by two games; beaten rivals Tennessee, Georgia, and Florida State; and won an Outback Bowl battle with Iowa before ranking No. 12 nationally in the final AP Top 25.

The Gators program appeared to be heading in the right direction. It would prove to be a championship foundation.

Much like his second seasons at Bowling Green and Utah, Meyer's encore at Florida featured no shortage of expectations. The Gators entered the 2006 campaign ranked No. 7 in the country. Not only did Florida return the core of its team from the season prior, with six returning starters on each side of the ball, but Meyer's No. 2 nationally ranked class in the 2006 recruiting cycle brought an additional infusion of talent.

While Leak resumed the role of starting quarterback as a senior, Meyer implemented a two-quarterback system that allowed him to use a five-star freshman named Tim Tebow as a situational signal-caller. Meanwhile, the nation's No. 2–ranked recruit, Percy Harvin, would find a home right away in Meyer's offense as a running back/wide receiver hybrid, accumulating 855 yards from scrimmage (428 rushing, 427 receiving) and five touchdowns as a true freshman.

It was Florida's upperclassmen, however, who provided Meyer's second Gators team with its true identity.

"It was a group of kids who struggled for a few years," Meyer recalled at Big Ten media days in 2012. "You come to places like Florida to go get a ring and they never had one. You can stoke that fire real easy."

The Gators won their first five games, the last of which was a top-10 matchup against LSU, which saw Tebow reenact Ben Moa's jump-pass touchdown from three years prior. Florida's victory over the No. 9 Tigers catapulted Meyer's squad to a No. 2 ranking, but the Gators wouldn't hold on to the spot for long. A week later, they'd suffer their first loss of the season, a 27–17 defeat at No. 11 Auburn.

Dropping to No. 9 and seemingly fading out of the national title picture, Florida then survived close contests against Georgia, Vanderbilt, South Carolina, and Florida State, clinching the SEC East and a spot in the conference title game against Arkansas.

Ranked No. 4 in the nation, the Gators' national title hopes were alive, but they'd need some help. And after beating the Razorbacks 38–28 in Atlanta, they'd receive just that in the form of a UCLA victory over No. 2 USC.

The final spot in the BCS Championship Game was up for grabs and came down to Florida and Michigan, which had lost its final game of the regular season to No. 1 Ohio State. After plenty of anticipation—and some campaigning from Meyer—the Gators would go on to jump the Wolverines in the final BCS rankings before postseason play, clinching a spot in the national title game against Meyer's former favorite team.

The Buckeyes had held on to the nation's top ranking from the pre-season all the way through the regular season, while Florida's spot in the national title game served as the subject of debate. Ohio State entered the game in Glendale, Arizona, as a one-touchdown favorite, as the crowning of the Buckeyes as national champions seemed more like inevitability.

But as the dust settled and the confetti fell from University of Phoenix Stadium, it was Meyer who was left lifting the crystal football. The Gators had not just beaten but manhandled the Buckeyes 41–14, sacking quarterback Troy Smith five times and allowing the Heisman Trophy winner to complete just four of his 14 pass attempts.

In just his second season, Meyer had returned Florida, which ranked in the top 10 nationally for the duration of the 2006 season, to the top of the college football world.

"My legacy was to get the University of Florida back here," Leak said after the game.

Meyer's legacy, meanwhile, was still just getting started.

Bringing back a significantly younger team than the season prior, the Gators entered the 2007 campaign ranked No. 6 in the nation. Consecutive top-10 losses to Auburn and LSU at the end of the first half of the season, however, brought Florida's hopes of repeating as national champions to an early end.

The Gators would go on to salvage the season, losing only one more regular season contest before losing to Michigan in the Citrus Bowl. That same year, Tebow became the third player in Florida history to win the Heisman Trophy.

While history will show Meyer's third season in Gainesville as a rebuilding year for the Gators, the following year would prove they were only reloading.

Bringing back eight starters on offense and nine on defense from its 9–4 2007 team, Florida appeared poised for another national title run at the start of the 2008 campaign. Tebow had emerged as one of college football's best players, Harvin already looked like a legitimate first-round

NFL draft pick, and Meyer had replenished his roster with the nation's top-ranked class in the 2007 recruiting cycle.

But after entering the season as the nation's No. 5–ranked team, the Gators' pursuit of another national title hit a snag in the fourth week of the season with a 31–30 loss at the hands of Ole Miss. Afterward, an

Meyer made the nation take notice when he began coaching at Florida. He led the Gators to national championship titles after the 2006 and 2008 seasons and finished his career at the program with a 5–1 record in bowl games.

emotional Tebow addressed the media, admitting that Florida's goal was indeed an undefeated season.

"I'm sorry. I'm extremely sorry. We were hoping for an undefeated season. That was my goal, something Florida's never done here," Tebow said. "But I promise you one thing: a lot of good will come out of this. You have never seen any player in the entire country play as hard as I will play the rest of this season and you'll never see someone push the rest of the team as hard as I will push everybody the rest of this season, and you'll never see a team play harder than we will the rest of this season. God Bless."

Tebow and the Gators would make good on what has since become immortalized as "the Promise." Winning its final eight games of the regular season—no margin of victory any smaller than 28 points—Florida reentered the national title picture, ranking No. 2 in the nation entering an SEC Championship Game against Nick Saban and Alabama. With a 31–20 victory over the Crimson Tide, the Gators clinched a spot in the BCS National Championship Game for the second time in three years.

Unlike two years prior, this time, Florida could no longer revel in being the underdog, as the top-ranked Gators entered the title game in Miami as a 5½-point favorite over No. 2 Oklahoma. It was a role that suited well what Meyer had built at Florida. With a 24–14 victory over the Sooners, the Gators cemented their spot atop the college football world as Meyer moved to the top of any legitimate "best coaches in college football" list.

With Tebow opting to forgo the NFL draft and return for his senior season, a burgeoning dynasty appeared to be growing in Gainesville. And, at least on the outside, it was showing no signs of slowing down.

Alluding back to his promise the season prior, Tebow—along with Meyer—made a mutual goal: the superstar signal-caller and now–living legend head coach wanted to put together the first undefeated season in Florida history. With two national titles in three seasons to their credit, it was all they had left.

"All we would talk about is, 'We have to be undefeated. We have to be undefeated,'" Meyer recalled to Dan Patrick in 2015.

Through 12 games, the Gators' goal was intact—although it was about as joyless an undefeated regular season as one could endure.

"We kind of drained the enjoyment out of it," Meyer said.

All that stood between No. 1 Florida and a defense of its national title was a rematch against Alabama in the SEC Title Game.

This time, however, it was the No. 2 Crimson Tide who would come out on top, stunning the Gators in a one-sided 32–13 blowout. Just like that, one dynasty was over and another had been jump-started.

For Meyer and Florida, the consequences would be further reaching.

Hours after the Gators' loss in the SEC title game, Meyer awoke with heart attack–like symptoms, which were later diagnosed as esophageal spasms. The stress of his job and his own obsessive nature had finally caught up to Meyer. The health scare was enough for him to announce an early retirement. He would later reveal that he had lost 37 pounds over the course of the 2009 campaign.

"I didn't want there to be a bad day where there were three kids sitting around wondering what to do next," Meyer told the *New York Times*. "It was the pattern of what I was doing and how I was doing it. It was self-destructive."

Meyer eventually rescinded his premature retirement plans, coaching Florida to a Sugar Bowl victory in Tebow's college finale and returning to the Gators sideline the following season. But the Florida program was hardly similar to what it had been even a year prior, when the Gators had compiled a 22-game winning streak over the course of two seasons.

With Tebow no longer in Gainesville and Meyer unsure how to coach and run a program at the only speed he had ever known, Florida struggled to a 7–5 regular record in 2010—Meyer's worst single season as a head coach.

Prior to the Gators' Outback Bowl victory over Penn State, Meyer once again resigned from Florida—this time for good—citing the desire to spend more time with his family.

His departure from college football wasn't without controversy. Over the course of his six seasons as Florida's head coach, 31 Gators players had been arrested, per the *New York Times*. Some in Gainesville still blame him for the quick deterioration of the Florida program, which has remained on the outside looking in to the national title picture since Meyer's departure.

Two years after being at the height of his profession, Meyer was a 46-year-old retiree with questions clouding his coaching future.

In 2011, he took a job at ESPN as a college football color commentator. His first assignment was to return to Columbus, where he'd cover Ohio State's season opener.

The Reinvention of Urban Meyer

Urban Meyer insists the plan was to stay away from coaching for as long as he could—or at least as long as it took to fix the health issues that plagued his final few years at Florida.

"In my mind I was convinced I was done coaching," Meyer said. "I was concerned with health issues. Family. I just wanted to be around them."

With Nicki now a Division I volleyball player at Georgia Tech and her younger sister, Gigi, not far behind at Florida Gulf Coast, Meyer would spend the first off-season of his early retirement watching his daughters play the sport they loved—in person—a luxury he hadn't previously been afforded over the course of his rigorous coaching career. Intermediately, Meyer helped out coaching his son Nate's youth baseball and football teams. Coaching never seemed to be far from his mind, but it was going to take an extraordinary set of circumstances to bring him back to a college sideline.

On Memorial Day 2011 such a situation arose. Amid allegations he had lied to the NCAA about violations committed by his players, Jim Tressel was forced to resign as Ohio State's head coach. One of Meyer's dream jobs was open.

Meyer would spend the 2011 season working in the commentary booth for ESPN, while Luke Fickell served as the Buckeyes' interim head coach. But as Ohio State faltered to a 6–6 regular season record, speculation only mounted, with Meyer's name being at the top of most lists when it came to who would be the Buckeyes' next head coach.

In the days leading up to Ohio State's regular season finale against Michigan—a game Meyer was originally scheduled to be on the call for—ESPN pulled Meyer from the broadcast. Two days after the Wolverines defeated the Buckeyes 40–34 to hand them their sixth loss of the season, Ohio State officially introduced Meyer as its 24th head coach in program history.

As Meyer reflected on his new gig, he recalled serving as an analyst for the Buckeyes' season opener against Akron, which marked his first time back in Ohio Stadium in over 20 years.

"I haven't been back since 1988," Meyer said. In that stadium against Akron—I'm up there with Chris [Spielman] and [ESPN play-by-play man] Dave Pasch, getting ready to broadcast that game, and that band came out of that tunnel, I was wiping tears out of my eyes and all the memories came back."

Inevitably, questions shifted to Meyer's health, given his messy exit from Florida a year prior.

"Healthwise I feel great," he insisted. "I had a health scare a couple of years ago that made me sit back, reflect. I didn't feel right. But I feel fantastic now.

"I just took that opportunity to do two things. First of all, get my health, get my family—I wanted to go spend time—I missed so much of them growing up. But I also went out and I researched and I spent time with colleagues, colleagues that I respect in this profession. And I don't want to be one of those guys that's sleeping in the office saying, 'I missed this, I missed that.' Believe it or not there's lot of quality coaches out there that are still able to have a little bit of balance. I was proud I had balance for quite a while. I lost that near the end. My health is in good shape."

In order to prove it, Meyer shared a contract drawn up by his daughter Nicki, which she wrote out on pink notebook paper. It included 10 promises:

1. My family will always come first.
2. I will take care of myself and maintain good health.
3. I will go on a trip once a year with Nicki—MINIMUM.
4. I will not go more than nine hours a day at the office.
5. I will sleep with my cell phone on silent.
6. I will continue to communicate daily with my kids.
7. I will trust God's plan and not be overanxious.
8. I will keep the lake house.
9. I will find a way to watch Nicki and Gigi play volleyball.
10. I will eat three meals a day.

"It's tougher than any other contract I've signed in my life," Meyer said. "So, yeah, a lot of thought. I don't want to spend all day talking about that, but I feel very blessed to be able to stand here, to know where I was and where I don't want to go again. And maybe help others."

It wouldn't take long for Meyer's new lifestyle to be put to the test.

In the midst of finalizing his coaching staff and putting together his first recruiting class at Ohio State, the Buckeyes were hit with a "sucker punch," as Meyer would call it. In his first season as the head coach at Ohio State, the Buckeyes would be ineligible for postseason play due to a one-year bowl ban that stemmed from the NCAA violations committed by Tressel and former Ohio State players.

As a result, seniors on the Buckeyes roster were free to transfer without punishment, potentially leaving an OSU roster already coming off its first losing season in 23 years in limbo.

Fortunately for Meyer, none of the Buckeyes' 21 returning seniors—including 11 starters—opted to take that opportunity. "We're very fortunate none did," Meyer said. "I have some incredible leaders on this team."

With Meyer likening the leadership of defensive end John Simon to Tim Tebow's at Florida, Ohio State embarked on a season unlike any other in program history, with "so-called nothing," as Meyer put it, to play for in terms of championships at the end of the year.

The Meyer era in Columbus got off to a strong start, with the Buckeyes beating Miami (Ohio) 56–10 in their 2012 season opener. It would take close calls, however, for the Buckeyes to survive against Central Florida, California, and Alabama Birmingham in the coming weeks, leaving a cloud of doubt over Ohio State entering Big Ten play.

"Obviously there's some growing pains," Meyer said following a 29–15 win over UAB to close out the nonconference portion of the Buckeyes' schedule. "I thought we'd be further ahead. It is what it is. We gotta get better and get better fast."

Little did Meyer know at the time that a turning point was around the corner.

In the days leading into Ohio State's Big Ten and road opener against Michigan State, Meyer sensed he wasn't receiving full buy-in from his new roster. So many of his players had been used to the old way the Buckeyes' program had been run and had yet to accept and trust their new coaching staff.

Meyer remembers the exact moment—to the minute—that all changed.

"September 29 at 11:22 [AM]," Meyer recalled. "I'm being serious."

"We had a meeting in a ballroom in East Lansing. Very intense, very emotional meeting. And what's when I saw it," he continued. "Up until then I didn't think we had them, to be honest with you. They weren't playing like it. And they weren't acting like it."

Following a toast with "championship" water in that very ballroom, the No. 14 Buckeyes gutted out a 17–16 win over the No. 20 Spartans thanks to a 63-yard pass from quarterback Braxton Miller to wide receiver Devin Smith late in the third quarter.

The following week, Ohio State fans got their first true taste of Meyer's high-powered offense with a 63–38 primetime win over Nebraska under the lights of Ohio Stadium. But as the Buckeyes cracked the top 10 of the AP poll and Miller morphed into a legitimate Heisman Trophy contender, the OSU defense continued to struggle in the midst of transition.

After surrendering 437 yards to the Cornhuskers, the Buckeyes allowed 511 yards—including 352 passing yards—in a 59–49 victory at Indiana.

Following the game, you wouldn't have known whether Ohio State had won or lost based on Meyer's tone.

"I'm not happy at all with what's going on defense. That includes players, coaches, and I think we can all get better," Meyer said. "It's a team effort. We've got good coaches, good players, and we'll move forward and get better."

Drawing back on his Bowling Green days, when position switches became the norm based on necessity, Meyer flipped senior fullback Zach Boren to the other side of the ball. As Ohio State's new starting middle linebacker, Boren helped stabilize an OSU defense that had routinely given up big plays in the first half of the 2012 season.

Urban Meyer was named the new head coach of the Ohio State Buckeyes on November 28, 2011. Through the 2016 season, he has amassed a 61–6 record with the program.

In the Buckeyes' final five games of the year, Ohio State surrendered an average of 20.4 points per game—more than four points fewer than its average through its first seven contests.

Meanwhile, Meyer's flair for the dramatic returned in the form of overtime victories over Purdue and Wisconsin to keep the Buckeyes' dreams of an undefeated season—and an outside shot at an AP national championship—alive.

Ohio State entered Meyer's first Michigan game with an 11–0 record intact, but would be without Simon, who suffered a shoulder injury during a four-sack performance against the Badgers the week prior.

Even without their senior leader on defense, the No. 4–ranked Buckeyes went on to earn a 26–21 win over the Wolverines, with fans flooding the field as Ohio State clinched its first undefeated season since 2002.

"Very emotional time. And obviously this is the state I grew up in," Meyer said afterward. "I made a comment on last November, December, whenever it was, that our objective is to make the great state of Ohio proud. I imagine tonight there's a lot of people in this great state very proud."

Alabama would go on to beat Notre Dame in the BCS National Championship Game, as the Buckeyes finished third in the final AP Top 25. The foundation for the Meyer era in Columbus, however, had been laid. And the Buckeyes' momentum would only continue in the coming year.

Returning 14 starters from the season prior, including the Big Ten's reigning MVP in Miller, an emerging star at running back in Carlos Hyde, All-American cornerback Bradley Roby, a future first-round pick at linebacker in Ryan Shazier, and four starting offensive linemen, the Buckeyes entered the 2013 season as the nation's consensus No. 2 team. Adopting "The Chase" as its battle cry early in the off-season, Ohio State appeared to be on a collision course with the defending national champion Crimson Tide.

And even with Miller missing the better part of three games early in the season with a knee injury, through 12 games, the Buckeyes lived up the hype. But as Ohio State extended its winning streak to a program record 24 games, an inconsistent Buckeyes defense once again reared its head. Those issues were particularly apparent in the passing game, where Ohio State ranked 112th nationally in passing yards allowed per game.

Yet there the Buckeyes were, undefeated and entering a Big Ten title game against Michigan State with a spot in the BCS National Championship Game on the line. Only, the Spartans passing attack would prove to be too much to overcome. After falling behind 17–0, Ohio State's second-half comeback fell short, with Michigan State ultimately pulling off the upset with a 34–24 win over the Buckeyes.

In an ensuing Orange Bowl appearance against Clemson, Ohio State's defensive passing game problems were once again exposed. En route to a 40–35 victory against the Buckeyes, Tigers quarterback Tajh Boyd threw for 378 yards and five touchdowns, with star receiver Sammy Watkins accounting for 16 receptions, 227 yards, and two scores.

After a 24–0 start to his Ohio State tenure, Meyer was in the midst of a two-game losing streak. Perhaps more alarmingly, something seemed to be broken when it came to his program's approach on the defensive side of the ball.

"We're not a championship-caliber defense right now," Meyer conceded after the game. "We've got to get better."

In order to accomplish that, Meyer brought in Chris Ash, who had previously served as the defensive coordinator at Arkansas and coached against the Buckeyes in the same capacity at Wisconsin in 2012. With another top-five recruiting class heavy on defensive talent, Ohio State's defense appeared to be taking the necessary steps forward.

Tougher challenges for the Buckeyes offense, however, would soon be on the horizon.

Although the Ohio State offense was replacing four starting offensive linemen, a running back who had just rushed for a combined 2,491 yards and 31 touchdowns in the previous two seasons in Hyde, and its leading receiver in Corey "Philly" Brown, the Buckeyes knew they had one player they could count on with the ball in his hands in Miller.

After winning a second consecutive Big Ten Silver Football, which the *Chicago Tribune* awards each year to the Big Ten's MVP, Miller toyed with entering the NFL draft but opted to return to school for his senior season following a shoulder injury suffered in the first quarter of the Orange Bowl.

Thanks in large part to Miller's presence, Ohio State entered the season ranked No. 5 in the AP Top 25. But the Buckeyes would never get to live up to that billing—at least not with Miller at the helm. Two weeks before the start of the 2014 season, Miller fell to the ground after throwing a short pass in practice. He had reinjured the same shoulder he had hurt against Clemson, only this time the prognosis was more serious. A torn labrum would keep Miller on the sideline for the entirety of Ohio State's upcoming season and ultimately end his career as a quarterback.

"Oh, it was devastating. It was a bad deal," Meyer said two days after the injury. "I didn't see exactly what happened and I thought someone hit him. I went berserk."

With a season opener against Navy fast approaching, the Buckeyes turned to a redshirt freshman quarterback named J.T. Barrett, who had yet to take an official snap in his college career and had just recently beaten out Cardale Jones for the right to be Miller's top understudy.

"It's a difficult part of the sport. It breaks your heart—I mean, like shatters your heart—but you gotta move on," Meyer said. "It's not hard to try and get the other guy ready and that's what we have to do."

Barrett was steady in the Buckeyes' season-opening 34–17 win over the Midshipmen, but his inexperience showed a week later against Virginia Tech, as the Hokies employed a cover-zero defense that dared the redshirt freshman to make a play with his arm downfield. Ohio State would lose the game 35–21—its third loss in the past four games—seemingly knocking the Buckeyes out of contention for a spot in the inaugural College Football Playoff a mere two weeks into the season.

Falling to No. 22 in the AP Top 25, Ohio State flew under the radar, but gained momentum in lopsided wins over Kent State, Cincinnati, Maryland, and Rutgers, scoring at least 50 points four weeks in a row. Most encouraging was the progress made by Barrett and several fellow members of the Buckeyes' 2013 class, including defensive end Joey Bosa, running back Ezekiel Elliott, linebacker Darron Lee, safety Vonn Bell, and cornerback Eli Apple.

"This is the most improved team I've ever been around," Meyer claimed.

After eking out a double-overtime victory on the road at Penn State, the Buckeyes were back in the playoff picture and after a 49–37 victory at No. 8 Michigan State on November 8, Ohio State appeared to regain control of its own destiny. Barrett, by this point, had become a full-fledged Heisman Trophy contender, ultimately finishing No. 5 in voting for the award behind Oregon quarterback Marcus Mariota, Wisconsin running back Melvin Gordon, Alabama wideout Amari Cooper, and Texas Christian quarterback Trevone Boykin.

With a 42–28 victory over Michigan, the Buckeyes clinched an 11–1 season record with an opportunity to potentially punch a ticket to the playoff ahead in the Big Ten title game. But when Barrett suffered a broken ankle in the third quarter against the Wolverines, Ohio State would find itself relying on a third-string quarterback in Jones to keep its postseason hopes alive.

The rest, as they say, is history.

Elliott's 696 rushing yards and eight touchdowns later, the Buckeyes had captured the first-ever College Football Playoff championship, knocking off the top three Heisman vote-getters in order to do so. It was the third national title of Meyer's coaching career, making him just the 15th head coach in college football history to have won as many and just the fourth since 1980.

This one, however, had additional sentimental value as it was the first he had won as a head coach in his home state.

"I'm not shy about the love I have for this great state," Meyer said. "Ashtabula, Ohio, is my hometown. I've [gotten] to travel all around the country and I realized how fortunate I am to grow up in a great town like that in a great state. I played college football here, and to bring now a national title to the great state of Ohio, it's almost surreal."

Three years after it looked like his coaching career might be over, Meyer was back on top of the college football world. More, he appeared set to continue to add to his legacy quickly, as the 2014 Buckeyes were ahead of schedule in their progression.

"We're losing some great seniors, but we have a lot of great young players that will step up," Elliott said ahead of the 2015 season. "This year was just a great year to learn a lot of things, and I think we'll be the same team next year."

From a roster standpoint, the Buckeyes were practically the same team—if not better. The first-ever unanimous No. 1 team in the preseason AP Top 25, Ohio State returned 14 starters from the season prior, including the preseason Heisman front-runner in Elliott and a unanimous All-American in Joey Bosa.

Having converted to wide receiver after taking a medical redshirt during the Buckeyes' run to a title, Miller also returned to the Ohio State lineup in 2015. In his first game back—a 42–24 win at Virginia Tech in front of a national audience—Miller totaled 140 yards and two touchdowns in his reintroduction to the college football world.

But while the Buckeyes possessed NFL draft prospects across their depth chart, one position remained unsettled. With Barrett once again healthy and Jones passing on entering the NFL draft, Meyer found himself with an unprecedented quarterback battle on his hands. One signal-caller had led Ohio State to the cusp of the College Football Playoff. The other had actually won it.

To their credit, all off-season, Meyer, Jones, and Barrett said all the right things. "It's the most refreshing competition I've ever witnessed," the Buckeyes head coach insisted.

When forced to pick, Meyer opted to stick with the hot hand, starting Jones in the Buckeyes' season opener against the Hokies. But Ohio State's passing game faltered and it wasn't long before he began calling on Barrett and his mobility in red-zone situations.

The Buckeyes won each of Jones' first six starts, but after Barrett totaled 132 yards and four touchdowns in a prime-time 38–10 win over Penn State, Meyer opted to make a lineup change. In a victory over Rutgers a week later, Ohio State's 2015 offense finally appeared to return to its 2014 form, with Barrett tallying 324 yards of total offense and five scores.

Only a week later, the Columbus Police would charge Barrett with operating a vehicle while impaired. Jones took over against Minnesota as Barrett served a one-game suspension, before Barrett returned to the starting lineup against Illinois a week later.

Simply put, despite having two qualified candidates, Meyer never seemed to find any stability at his most important position throughout the 2015 season—at least not before it was too late.

In an ugly 17–14 loss to Michigan State on senior day in the second-to-last week of the regular season, the Buckeyes national-title defense came to an abrupt end. Barrett completed just 9-of-16 pass attempts for 46 yards. But Ohio State's passing woes were overshadowed by the performance of Elliott, who received just 12 carries against the Spartans.

After the game, the Buckeyes' star running back ripped his coaching staff's play-calling and announced his intentions to enter the upcoming NFL draft.

"I'm disappointed in the play-calling. I'm disappointed in the situations that we were put in, and I wish it all played out differently," Elliott said. "We weren't put in the right situations to win this game."

Less than a year after winning the national title, Meyer appeared to have lost his locker room. A highly anticipated matchup with Michigan and first-year Wolverines head coach Jim Harbaugh loomed and Ohio State's once-promising season seemed to be heading off the rails.

The Buckeyes, however, not only bounced back, but finally played to their potential, beating Michigan 42–13 before topping Notre Dame 44–28 in a Fiesta Bowl finale.

Four months later, the 2015 Ohio State squad added to its legacy with 12 players selected in the NFL draft, including five first-round picks. But when it comes to their on-field accomplishments, despite their 12–1 record, 2015 will always be remembered as a season of what could have been for the Buckeyes.

The heavy turnover on the OSU roster—including nine early entrants into the NFL draft—also left Meyer with the most uncertainty he's faced entering a season since arriving in Columbus.

Yet despite returning just three starters on each side of the ball, the Buckeyes got off to a fast start in 2016, which was highlighted by a 45–24 win at No. 14 Oklahoma in the third week of the season. Behind steady play from Barrett, the emergence of H-back Curtis Samuel, and one of the nation's top defenses, Ohio State quickly rose to No. 2 in the polls before suffering a 24–21 defeat at the hands of Penn State in its seventh game of the season.

The Buckeyes, however, remained in the national title picture and climbed back to No. 2 in the playoff rankings prior to a narrow 17–16 win against Michigan State in a windy East Lansing in the second-to-last week of the regular season.

That set up a historic No. 2 vs. No. 3 matchup between Ohio State and Michigan, with a spot in the College Football Playoff seemingly on the line. After falling behind 17–7, the Buckeyes bounced back with a fourth-quarter comeback, forcing an overtime on a Tyler Durbin 23-yard field goal with one second left.

Two overtime periods, one controversial fourth-down spot, and a 15-yard Samuel scamper later and Ohio State had successfully beaten the Wolverines for a fifth straight time under Meyer, punching its ticket to the College Football Playoff in the process.

"That is one of the classic games of this rivalry that will forever be, because I know this rivalry as well as anybody," Meyer said afterward. "I'm not saying it's the greatest, because that's disrespectful for the other players that have played in it. But that's an instant classic between two great teams. We knew going in it was going to be that way."

The Buckeyes'—and Meyer's—bid for another national title, however, would fall short. An Ohio State passing attack that had sputtered down the stretch once again struggled in what became a lopsided 31–0 loss to eventual national champion Clemson in the College Football Playoff semifinal Fiesta Bowl.

In the weeks following the Buckeyes' season-ending loss, Meyer made adjustments to his coaching staff, bringing on former Indiana head coach Kevin Wilson as Ohio State's new offensive coordinator and NFL assistant Ryan Day as its new quarterbacks coach.

The Buckeyes had crashed college football's final four in what was supposed to be a rebuilding season for Ohio State, but Meyer wasn't satisfied.

"Our anticipation is to get back here next year," Meyer said after the Fiesta Bowl, "and take a good swing at it."

In his first five seasons with the Buckeyes, Meyer made his expectations clear and it's the same standard he's held throughout his 15-year coaching career.

Nothing less than championship caliber will do.

PART II

★ ★ ★

Urban Meyer vs. His Rivals

Urban Meyer may not be a big personality—in fact, he's become pretty well versed in "coach speak" over the course of his career—but as one of college football's most prominent figures, he's inevitably been linked to and compared with several coaches across the country in his time in the public spotlight.

Sometimes, Meyer's feuds—or perceived feuds—have come by way of predetermined on-field rivalries, while others have been the result of public spats (often stemming from the recruiting trail). But regardless of the reason for their existence, no coach in college football has seemingly been involved in more rivalries over the course of his career—not that Meyer has seemed to mind.

In fact, regardless which of the four stops in his head-coaching career he's been at, Meyer has relished being a part of each school's respective rivalries. Even to this day, he won't even say some of the schools' names.

"You go to Bowling Green, we certainly didn't invent that rivalry [vs. Toledo]," Meyer said recalled in 2014. "And we go to Utah and once again we didn't invent the rivalry [vs. BYU]. We maybe put a lot of emphasis on it, called them 'the Team Down South,' and had some success out there with it.

"Then we go to Florida. Interesting at Florida, you have three of them; you have Tennessee early in the year. You have Georgia, and you have 'the Team Out West' [Florida State]. And some people say we're going to have fun—I told you, there's no fun in a rivalry unless you're singing the fight song after the game."

With a career record of 26–3 in rivalry games, Meyer has sung plenty of fight songs over the course of his four coaching stops. In fact, you'd have to go back to Florida's loss to Florida State at the end of the 2010 season to find the last time he lost such contest.

Now that you know Meyer's story, let's take a look at how it stacks up to those of his peers. There may not be a better way to truly grasp Meyer's dominance than to compare it to those he's crossed paths in his coaching career.

★ ★ ★

Urban Meyer vs. Bobby Bowden

If you were first introduced to Meyer upon his arrival at Florida, the first rivalry you likely remember him being a part of is the Gators' annual Sunshine Showdown with Florida State.

Only, when it came to Meyer's five matchups with legendary Seminoles head coach Bobby Bowden, there wasn't much of a rivalry to be had—at least not on the field. From 2005 to 2009, Meyer's Gators laid claim to a 5–0 record versus 'That Team Out West," outscoring Florida State by a combined total of 182–58.

Despite the lopsided scoreboards, the five late-November matchups and postgame handshakes between Meyer and Bowden remained both highly anticipated and memorable nonetheless. That's because, in many ways, Bobby Bowden was to the 1990s what Meyer had become to the mid-2000s.

A native of Birmingham, Alabama, Bowden's ascent up the coaching ranks began in the mid-1950s, when he got his first gig as the offensive coordinator at his alma mater, Howard (now known as Samford), where he played running back after transferring from Alabama's freshman team following the 1948 season.

In 1955, South Georgia State College hired Bowden not only as its football coach, but as the junior college's baseball coach, basketball coach, and athletic director. After SGSC ended its football program following the 1958 season, Bowden returned to Howard, where, as the head coach of the Bulldogs, he compiled a 31–6 record from 1959 to '62.

Florida State head coach Bill Peterson hired Bowden as his wide receivers coach in 1963, and Bowden spent three seasons in Tallahassee before taking over as the offensive coordinator at West Virginia in 1966. When Mountaineers head coach Jim Carlen left to for the same role at Texas Tech following the 1969 campaign, West Virginia promoted Bowden to head coach.

In six seasons with the Mountaineers, Bowden compiled a 42–26 record, including a victory in the Peach Bowl at the end of the 1975 campaign, which secured WVU just its second top-20 finish in 20 years. After the season, Florida State hired Bowden as its head coach following a 4–29 run from 1973 to '75.

In his 2010 book, *Called to Coach: Reflections on Life, Faith, and Football*, Bowden conceded he only took the Seminoles job for the warmer weather and didn't intend to stay in Tallahassee long.

"The Florida State program was in disarray and had not been very good in a long time," Bowden wrote. "Honestly, the Seminoles were really that bad in football at the time."

With Bowden on the sideline, that didn't last for long.

After compiling a 5–6 debut season at Florida State, Bowden's teams would go on to win at least 10 games in three of the next four years. By the late 1980s, the Seminoles were routinely compiling wins in the double digits, major bowl victories, and top-five finishes, a trend that would only continue as the Independent program joined the Atlantic Coast Conference.

In 1993, Florida State won its first national championship and laid claim to its first Heisman Trophy winner in quarterback Charlie Ward. After originally thinking he would leave Tallahassee in order to take over a more storied program like Alabama, Louisiana State University, or even a job in the NFL, Bowden had created his own history—and he wasn't done yet.

Bowden and the Seminoles won their second national title in 1999, fittingly making them the last champion of the decade. No college football program dominated the 1990s—or any other decade in the modern era, for that matter—like Florida State did, compiling a 109–13–1 overall record, the most victories by any team over the course of a decade. When it comes to winning percentage, the Seminoles' 88.6 percent mark from 1990 to '99 is topped only by Oklahoma's 89.5 percent success rate in the 1950s.

Florida State may never have won back-to-back national championships, but make no mistake; no program in college football is more deserving of being called a "dynasty" than the 1990s Seminoles.

"You have to do it year after year after year," Bowden said, per ESPN's Mark Schlabach. "That's what makes a dynasty. You can't do it in two years. You can't do it in three years. It has to be for a long time."

On top of his on-field success, Bowden helped transform Tallahassee into arguably the first modern NFL draft factory. Florida State had at least one player picked every year from 1984 to 2009. Over the course of Bowden's Seminoles career, 182 former FSU players were drafted by NFL teams, including nearly 30 first-round picks and notable names such as Deion Sanders, Derrick Alexander, Derrick Brooks, Peter Boulware, Walter Jones, Warrick Dunn, Peter Warrick, and Anquan Boldin. Bowden even helped a kicker get picked in the first round, when the Oakland Raiders selected Sebastian Janikowski with the No. 17 overall pick in the 2000 NFL draft.

In his time in Tallahassee, Bowden coached 24 consensus All-Americans and, in 2000, quarterback Chris Weinke became his and the program's second Heisman Trophy winner. That same season, the Seminoles fell short in their attempt to repeat as national champions, losing to Oklahoma in the Orange Bowl, which doubled as that season's BCS national title game.

From 1987 to 2000, the Seminoles enjoyed 14 consecutive 10-win seasons and an NCAA-record 14 straight top-five finishes. In 2001, however, Florida State fell to 8–4 and would only enjoy one more top-10 finish under the direction of Bowden, in 2003.

As the Seminoles' descent into mediocrity in the late 2000s coincided with Meyer's peak in Gainesville, Florida State president T.K. Wetherell forced Bowden into an early retirement. He retired with 357 career wins—the second most in college football history—although the NCAA officially recognizes his career record as 346–123–4 due to wins vacated from the use of ineligible players in 2006 and 2007.

When it comes to comparing legacies, Bowden and Meyer's respective longevity makes it tough to do. Bowden spent 40 years as the head coach of a major college football program, including 34 seasons as Florida State's head coach. Meyer is just now preparing to enter his 16th season as a head coach, his sixth season at Ohio State tying his tenure at Florida for his longest stint at a single school.

Nevertheless, Meyer has already won more national titles in his career than Bowden and his .851 career winning percentage dwarfs his former rival's mark of .740, even when including Bowden's vacated victories. It's also conceivable that Meyer, who currently lays claim to 10 double-digit win seasons in his 15-year career, could eventually catch Bowden's mark of 18 10-win seasons.

It's unlikely, however, Meyer will ever catch many of Bowden's other lofty career numbers.

While Meyer's nine career bowl victories are good for the 14th most in college football history, they still trail Bowden's 22, which are the second most ever in the history of the sport. Over the course of his career, Bowden led West Virginia and Florida State to a combined 33 bowl games, while Meyer has combined for 12 bowl appearances—including two in the 2015 College Football Playoff—throughout his time at Utah, Florida, and Ohio State.

As far as individual accomplishments are concerned, Meyer's had tallied 11 consensus All-Americans over the course of his career at the end of the 2016 season, trailing Bowden's 24. Following the 2016 NFL draft, Meyer's programs had produced a combined 61 NFL draft picks under his watch—just a little more than a third of the 182 players Bowden's teams put in the pros.

Because of the amount of time each spent coaching—and especially because one of their coaching careers is still ongoing—it's difficult to truly measure what Bowden accomplished against what Meyer is in the midst of accomplishing. It's not, however, hard to see that at each of their respective peaks, these were two of the most dominant coaches in all of college football.

In the same vein in which Bowden dominated the 1990s, Meyer dominated the 2000s—albeit at three different programs. From his first season as a head coach in 2001 to the end of the decade in 2009, Meyer accumulated a combined record of 96–18. Those 96 wins would have been the 10th most of any single program throughout the entire 2000s—and that's without an entire season as a head coach in 2000 to Meyer's credit.

Unsurprisingly, both the *Sporting News* and ESPN named Meyer their "Coach of the Decade" for the 2000s.

Unfortunately for college football fans, the intersection of the two living legends' paths came at very different points in their respective careers.

In 2005—Meyer's first season at Florida—both the Gators and Seminoles entered the annual Sunshine Showdown ranked inside the AP Top 25. But you wouldn't know No. 19 Florida and No. 23 Florida State were on perceived equal footing on that late-November afternoon, with the Gators trouncing the Seminoles 34–7 behind 211 passing yards and a pair of touchdown throws from quarterback Chris Leak. Meanwhile, Meyer's defense limited FSU quarterback Drew Weatherford to completing just 24 of his 42 pass attempts and the Seminoles defense to just 49 rushing yards on 28 attempts on the day.

The following year, however, would see a closer call occur between the two teams, even with Florida possessing a 10–1 record and in search of a BCS title-game berth and Florida State in the midst of what would be its first .500 regular season record since Bowden's first year in Tallahassee. With the game tied at 14 early in the fourth quarter, Leak directed a 10-play, 74-yard drive, finding wide receiver Dallas Baker for a 25-yard touchdown and the game's go-ahead score.

With 283 passing yards and two touchdowns to his credit, Leak's performance against the Seminoles went a long way toward proving he was indeed a championship-caliber quarterback—something Bowden alluded to in his postgame press conference.

"They looked darn second to that 1996 (national championship) team they had," Bowden said, per the Associated Press. "That's how they looked to me. So much skill running around out there you have to be able to contain them all day long. If they didn't have such a good quarterback that can get them the ball, then we could have handled it.

"Their quarterback can do it."

In 2007, Florida returned to its dominant ways over its in-state rival, scoring touchdowns on four of its first five possessions and amassing 541 total yards en route to a 45–12 victory. With 351 total yards and five touchdowns to his credit in the Gators' regular season finale, Tim Tebow put the final touches on his Heisman Trophy–winning campaign.

The rivalry would remain one-sided a season later, as Florida steamrolled the Seminoles 45–15. As a team, Florida compiled 317 rushing yards and allowed Florida State to complete just 10 of its 32 pass attempts as it extended its winning streak on the season to eight games in what would be Meyer's second national championship season with the Gators.

"It was a good tail-whipping," Bowden said afterward, per the AP. "I didn't think they would beat us like that here. The last time we had a beating like that was last year against them."

The 2009 meeting between Florida and Florida State would serve as both Tebow's senior day with the Gators and Bowden's regular season finale for the Gators. And for the sixth season in a row, it was Florida who came out on top, with a 37–10 victory thanks to 311 yards and five touchdowns from its senior quarterback.

After the game, Bowden insisted he wanted to return to the sideline for 2010, but also admitted he had some "soul-searching" to do. Three days later, the Hall of Fame head coach announced his retirement after 34 seasons with the Seminoles, capping his legendary career with a victory over his former employer, West Virginia, in the Gator Bowl.

When it comes to comparisons with Meyer, Bowden will always hold an advantage when it comes to longevity. Meyer, however, arguably reached a higher peak since extending the prime of his coaching career throughout his time at Ohio State.

But regardless of whose legacy you prefer, there's no denying the similarities between the onetime rivals, who happen to be two of the best to ever do it in college football history. At least as far as Meyer's concerned, Bowden's legacy is one that won't ever be replicated.

"At one school and that long a career in this day and age? You just won't see it," Meyer said upon Bowden's retirement. "You just admire a guy that had the stamina and did it the right way. That's the thing you always admire about Coach Bowden. He's always done it the right way.

"I'm good friends with Coach Bowden, and I have a lot of respect for him…he's great for college football."

Urban Meyer vs. Bob Stoops

After returning from his one-season sabbatical between stints at Florida and Ohio State, Meyer often referenced the need to find balance between his professional and personal lives.

In doing so, Meyer always seemed to have a specific example ready to cite.

"I went on a yearlong research project. How can you do both?" Meyer told ESPN's Wright Thompson in 2012. "How does Bob Stoops be a good dad and husband and still have success?"

Meyer would later reveal that during his year away from coaching, he met with the former Oklahoma coach on at least one occasion to see how he maintains his personal and professional balance. In 2016, a week before Meyer's Buckeyes faced Stoops' Sooners, Stoops confirmed the meeting.

"We talked," Stoops said, per the *Tulsa World*. "It wouldn't be for me to speak on. But I've been comfortable overall with the balance of my life and the way I've gone about it. Urban has a great family and he's done a super job everywhere he's been, and he's a good guy when you visit with him."

Before 2011, Meyer admitted his relationship with Stoops was purely professional, having since grown into a friendly kinship between two Ohio-born head coaches. In 2013, Meyer even stated that it was Stoops who first urged the Buckeyes head coach to join Twitter. Reluctantly, Meyer obliged.

It's unsurprising Meyer would put so much stock into Stoops' advice. Two of the most successful coaches of the last two decades, Meyer's and Stoops' respective careers have often followed parallel paths and have, on occasion, intersected.

Bob Stoops was practically born into coaching. The son of Ron Stoops Sr., Bob spent his high school career playing for his father, who was the defensive coordinator at Ohio prep powerhouse Youngstown Cardinal Mooney. After a standout career with the Cardinals, Stoops earned a scholarship to play safety at Iowa, where he served as a four-year starter. The Hawkeyes' team MVP in 1982, Stoops finished his career with 205 tackles, 10 interceptions, and two All–Big Ten selections. To this day, he is still routinely considered one of the hardest-hitting players in Iowa football history.

Stoops' time as a player in Iowa City coincided with the arrival of legendary head coach Hayden Fry and in Stoops' junior season, the Hawkeyes won the Big Ten and clinched their first Rose Bowl appearance in 23 years. After his playing career came to an end, Stoops immediately joined Fry's staff as a graduate assistant. In 1983, he was part of a staff that also included future head coaches Kirk Ferentz, Barry Alvarez, Dan McCarney, and Bill Snyder.

"For sure, you could tell they were all pretty special on that staff," Stoops told ESPN.com's Brian Bennett in 2015. "And I always felt incredibly lucky and blessed that I was able to hang around them all."

After spending five seasons as an assistant at his alma mater, Stoops briefly returned to Northeast Ohio, where he served as an assistant coach at Kent State under head coach Dick Crum in 1988.

In 1989, Kansas State hired Snyder as its head coach and the former Iowa offensive coordinator and quarterbacks coach would bring on Stoops to coach the Wildcats' defensive backs.

While in Manhattan, Stoops helped oversee one of the most dramatic turnarounds in college football history. After winning a combined four games from 1985 to '89, including winless seasons in 1987 and 1988, the Wildcats compiled a 7–4 record in 1991—Stoops' first season as Kansas State's defensive coordinator. With Stoops overseeing their defense, the Wildcats compiled a combined 28–7–1 record from 1993 to 1995, earning three consecutive bowl appearances after a 10-year absence from postseason play.

In 1996, Florida head coach Steve Spurrier hired Stoops as his new defensive coordinator after the Gators surrendered 62 points to Nebraska in the Fiesta Bowl at the end of the 1995 campaign.

It didn't take long for Stoops to help turn the Florida defense around. The Gators defense ranked No. 14 nationally in total defense and No. 15 in scoring as Florida won the national championship in Stoops' first season in Gainesville.

He'd spend two more years at Florida, with the Gators defense ranking No. 12 in 1997 and No. 9 in 1998. All of 38 years old, Stoops had become one of the hottest assistant coaches in all of college football.

As it became clear he was primed for a head coaching job, two front-runners emerged in the race for Stoops' services: his alma mater, Iowa, and the more historic Oklahoma.

A week after Fry's retirement, Stoops appeared destined to return to Iowa City. The *Gainesville Sun* even ran a report announcing the

Hawkeyes' expected hiring of Stoops, which included a timetable and salary figures, per the *Daily Iowan*.

Former Iowa AD Bob Bowlsby, however, denied the report as talks between the two camps stalled. The Hawkeyes had committed to interviewing Ferentz.

"All of the interviews took place over six or seven days; it was a pretty crazy chase for a while there," Bowlsby said, per the *Daily Iowan*.

On December 1, 1998, Stoops accepted a job to become the next head coach of the Sooners.

One day later, Iowa would announce Ferentz as its official hire.

The two former Fry assistants have since become the two longest-tenured active coaches in college football—with Stoops maintaining a one-day advantage in his hiring.

In Norman, Stoops had his work cut out for himself as he took over a once-proud program. Throughout its history, Oklahoma had claimed six national titles under the direction of coaching legends Bud Wilkinson and Barry Switzer, but had since fallen on hard times, having gone five consecutive seasons without a winning record, including a combined 12–22 record in three seasons from 1996 to 1998 under the direction of John Blake.

Much like at his previous stops as a defensive coordinator, the Sooners would enjoy a quick turnaround with Stoops at the helm. In 1999, Oklahoma compiled a 7–5 record, including an impressive 51–6 win over then–No. 13 Texas A&M. It was the start of a turnaround.

As for the return to prominence Sooners fans had been hoping for? That would come a year later.

Oklahoma entered the new millennium ranked No. 19 nationally and with expectations for the first time in nearly a decade. The Sooners would get off to a strong start to the 2000 season, scoring at least 42 points in each of their first three games before beating Kansas 34–16 in their Big 12 opener.

It was in the Red River Shootout, however, that Oklahoma made its first true statement under Stoops. In the Sooners' annual rivalry game against Texas, which the Longhorns had won eight of the prior 10 meetings of, including each of the previous three, No. 10 Oklahoma took No. 11 Texas to the woodshed with a 63–14 blowout. A week later, Stoops' team would knock off his former employer, No. 2 Kansas State, which the No. 3 Sooners followed with a 31–14 win over top-ranked Nebraska.

Now the nation's No. 1 team, Oklahoma survived a close call in the Bedlam series against Oklahoma State in its regular season finale a week before beating Kansas State 27–24 in a rematch in the Big 12 Championship Game.

With an offense and defense that each ranked in the nation's top 10 by season's end, the Sooners then captured their seventh national championship in program history with a 13–2 win over Florida State in the Orange Bowl.

"To be honest with you, we fully expected to play that way," Stoops said after the game, per the AP. "And as a team, we expected to win.

"Our players recognize that the history of Oklahoma is winning championships. We already had six, now we have seven."

In just his second season as a head coach, Stoops had recorded an undefeated 13–0 season and captured a national championship—the second on his résumé including his 1996 title with the Gators. More important, he had helped restore glory to one of college football's most historic programs.

"It's easy to say," Stoops said, "Oklahoma is back."

By any reasonable metric, what would follow would be one of the most successful eras in Sooners history.

With Stoops' recruiting gaining steam, Oklahoma won at least 11 games in each of the following four seasons, winning two Big 12 titles and playing for the BCS National Championship at the end of the 2003 and 2004 seasons. In 2003, Sooners quarterback Jason White became the fourth player in program history to win the Heisman Trophy, throwing for 3,846 yards and 40 touchdowns while leading Oklahoma to a 12–2 record.

The Sooners signal-caller would return to Norman for his senior season in 2004, but finished third in the Heisman race behind winner and USC quarterback Matt Leinart and his own Oklahoma teammate, freshman running back Adrian Peterson.

The nation's top-ranked prospect in the 2004 class, Peterson would enjoy a storied career in his time as a Sooner, rushing for 4,041 yards and 41 touchdowns in three seasons. The eventual seven-time Pro Bowl selection is one of many future NFL stars Stoops has helped produce in his time in Norman, a list that also includes the likes of safety Roy Williams, defensive tackle Tommie Harris, offensive tackle Jammal Brown, offensive lineman David Joseph, defensive tackle Gerald McCoy, offensive tackle Trent Williams, tight end Jermaine Gresham, and running back DeMarco Murray. As of the 2016 NFL draft, Stoops' Sooners program has produced 81 NFL draft picks.

In 2008, quarterback Sam Bradford, whom the St. Louis Rams would select first overall in the 2010 draft, became Oklahoma's fifth and Stoops' second Heisman Trophy winner.

All that talent resulted in an unsurprising string of success for the Sooners under Stoops. In 2013, he surpassed Switzer for the most wins in Oklahoma history. His 14 10-win seasons are the most of any college football coach since 2000. In 18 years, he's amassed a career 190–48 record and won 10 Big 12 titles. His 160 wins were the most of any college football coach in his first 15 seasons as a head coach.

Until Meyer broke his mark with 165 victories in his first 15 years.

While Stoops has been a model of consistency—and at a high level—over the course of his career, his peaks have never reached the same heights that Meyer has. Although he has kept the Sooners at the forefront of the national title race on an almost annual basis, his national championship record is limited to 1–3.

The most recent of Oklahoma's national championship defeats came at the hands of Meyer, who won his second national championship with Florida against the Sooners in the BCS National Championship Game in Miami at the end of the 2008 season. The Gators had plowed through the second half of their schedule, but found a tough test in Oklahoma, which in addition to Bradford possessed one of the game's great defensive minds in Stoops.

In the first half, the Sooners stifled the Gators with an unexpected 3–4 defensive front as the two teams headed to the locker rooms at half-time tied at 7.

"That's one of the first times that—that's one of those sick feelings on the sidelines," Meyer recalled. "I used language I can't use right here, like son of a…it's tough."

After Florida took a 14–7 lead in the third quarter on a Percy Harvin two-yard touchdown, Oklahoma tied the game early in the fourth quarter when Bradford found Gresham for an 11-yard score. The Gators, however, would regain the lead on a 27-yard Jonathan Phillips field goal and seal the contest when Tebow connected with wideout David Wilson for a four-yard touchdown with 3:07 left in the game.

"First-class outfit, first-class university, the way their players played," Meyer said of Oklahoma afterward. "I've known Coach Stoops—probably known of him longer than I've known him. But I think that was a great college football game between two very well-coached teams and two classy outfits. If you're a fan watching college football, it's all good, watching that game."

Meyer appeared to be in the midst of a budding dynasty, but just two years later, he found himself on a flight to Norman to visit Stoops. In addition to being a model of consistency on the field, Stoops has been one off it as well, which is something Meyer has attempted to emulate since his return to the coaching ranks.

When comparing the legacies of the two, it's tough not to give Meyer the edge. Meyer's 10–3 record in bowl games trumps Stoops' 9–9 mark, which is a part of the reason some sarcastically dubbed the former long-time Sooners head coach "Big Game Bob."

Meyer has more national titles; a higher winning percentage; and also won each of two head-to-head matchups against Stoops, including a 45–21 Ohio State victory over Oklahoma in the third week of the 2016 regular season.

But regardless of how their records—or résumés—stack up against one another on the field, Meyer and Stoops clearly share an immense respect for one another off of it. As two coaching titans of the 2000s and beyond, they'll inevitably—or perhaps, continually—be linked throughout the duration of their respective careers.

★ ★ ★

Urban Meyer vs. Dabo Swinney

Clemson's Delta airliner had barely landed at Phoenix Sky Harbor International Airport by the time Dabo Swinney paid his first compliment to Urban Meyer in the days leading up to the 2016 College Football Playoff semifinal Fiesta Bowl.

"I've got a lot of respect for Coach Meyer. He barely ever loses," Swinney said. "We were joking back in Clemson that it's like Knute Rockne and Urban Meyer as the two winningest coaches ever."

The Tigers head coach wasn't done there. Swinney also stated that he had bought a copy of Meyer's 2015 book, *Above the Line*, in an effort to scour it for details regarding the Buckeyes' possible game plan.

"I'll have to get that thing read by the end of week," Swinney said. "If y'all got the CliffsNotes, send them my way."

By the end of the week, Swinney insisted those CliffsNotes would no longer be necessary.

"I read that in your book, by the way," he told Meyer at the final pre-game press conference. "Awesome, four-to-six (seconds), A-to-B. Nine units. I'm getting it."

Whether or not Swinney had actually read Meyer's autobiography or was just busting his chops remains unclear. But Clemson did seem to hold every advantage it possibly could over Ohio State just a day later, as the Tigers handed the Buckeyes their worst defeat of the Meyer era with a 31–0 shutout in the College Football Playoff semifinal.

In fact, it was the worst loss of Meyer's coaching career, period, and marked the first time any of his teams in 15 years as a head coach had ever been shut out. The victory advanced the Tigers to the College

Football Playoff Championship Game and Swinney to 2–0 in his career against Meyer—a mark matched only by former Auburn coach Tommy Tubberville until his Cincinnati team lost to Ohio State in 2014.

Yet while Swinney may have gotten the best of Meyer in their two head-to-head matchups, coaching legacies are defined by more than just two games. And in many ways, when it comes to Swinney's, his story is just beginning.

Born William Christopher Swinney, but nicknamed "Dabo" because his older brother Tripp referred to him as "that boy," Dabo spent the first 31 years of his life either around or a part of Alabama football. Born in Birmingham, but raised in Pelham—just an hour outside of Tuscaloosa—Swinney was raised as a devout fan of Bear Bryant's Crimson Tide thanks to his father, Ervil.

"My dad was the biggest Alabama fan ever, and I was brainwashed," Swinney told ESPN's Mark Schlabach in 2016. "In Alabama, when you come out of the hospital, they have to stamp your birth certificate with either Alabama or Auburn, or you don't leave."

After a tough upbringing, which included Ervil's bout with alcoholism, Tripp suffering from memory loss after a severe car accident, and relatively little income, Swinney enrolled at Alabama in 1988. After his first fall on campus, he opted to walk on to Gene Stallings' football team, scraping together just enough money to remain enrolled for the 1989 season.

After spending a year on the Crimson Tide scout team as a wide receiver, Stallings elevated Swinney to travel squad in 1990 and awarded him with a scholarship in 1991. By the time his Alabama career had come to an end, Swinney had recorded seven catches for 81 yards and was a member of Alabama's 1992 national title team.

"He was an average player," Stallings said, per Schlabach. "He wanted to be a great player, but he just wasn't blessed with a lot of talent. He had a lot of heart."

After graduating with a degree in commerce and business administration, Swinney joined Stallings' staff as a graduate assistant. In 1996, he was promoted to wide receivers/tight ends coach and remained on Mike DuBose's staff, first as a tight ends coach in 1997, before taking over the wide receivers on a full-time basis in 1998.

Meyer and his contemporary, Dabo Swinney, faced off in the 2014 Orange Bowl, in which Swinney's Clemson Tigers defeated Meyer's Ohio State Buckeyes 40–35.

While serving as an assistant in Tuscaloosa, Swinney helped develop tight end Patrick Hape and wide receivers Freddie Milons and Jason McAddley into future NFL draft picks. After a 3–8 season in 2000, however, Alabama let go of DuBose and his staff.

Swinney then spent the next two years out of coaching, instead working at AIG Baker Real Estate on development projects. In 2002, his former position coach with the Crimson Tide, Terry Bowden, took over as the head coach at Clemson and hired Swinney as his wide receivers coach and recruiting coordinator.

As he did at Alabama, Swinney thrived as a player developer, with Tigers wideouts Derrick Hamilton (2004), Airese Currie (2005), and Chansi Stuckey (2007) each being selected in the NFL draft under his watch. In 2007, Aaron Kelly caught 88 passes for 1,081 yards and 11 touchdowns before finishing his career with 232 total receptions—the most in ACC history at the time.

But while Swinney consistently provided Clemson with valuable targets in the passing game, it was on the recruiting trail that he truly made his presence felt. Over the course of his tenure as the Tigers' recruiting coordinator, Swinney played a key role in helping Clemson land high-level prospects such as 5-star defensive end Da'Quan Bowers, 5-star defensive end Ricky Sapp, and 4-star quarterback Tajh Boyd. Swinney also served as the Tigers' primary recruiter of 5-star running back C.J. Spiller in the 2006 recruiting cycle and was named one of Rivals.com's top 25 recruiters in 2007 for his efforts.

But as Swinney's status in coaching circles grew, Clemson failed to meet on-field expectations, with Bowden resigning following a 3–3 start in 2008 after the Tigers entered the year ranked No. 9 nationally. Amid no shortage of uncertainty surrounding its program, Clemson promoted Swinney as its interim head with no guarantee he would hold the position past the second half of the 2008 campaign.

But with six games left in front of him, Swinney made the most of his opportunity as the Tigers won four of their final five regular season games, including a 31–14 win over rival South Carolina to clinch a New Year's Day Gator Bowl bid.

Two days after beating the Gamecocks—and following a more-than-monthlong national search—Clemson removed the interim tag from Swinney's title.

"Under some difficult circumstances, Dabo did a real good job of salvaging that season and I kept coming back to him," then–Clemson Athletic Director Terry Don Phillips said per the *Greenville News*. "I had seen the situation he'd been placed in, how he handled it, how the kids reacted to him, the gain in attendance, the way he organized things. It was small things like that, cumulatively, that made me believe he could do it."

Phillips would be rewarded for his faith—and then some.

In Swinney's first season as the Tigers' full-time head coach, Clemson clinched a spot in the ACC title game, but would lose 39–34 to Georgia Tech, a victory that the Yellow Jackets have since vacated due to NCAA violations. Two years later, the Tigers would win their first conference title in 20 years with a 38–10 win over Virginia Tech for the ACC championship.

Clemson would go on to lose 70–33 to West Virginia in the Orange Bowl, but amassed a combined 36–18 record and three top-five finishes in Swinney's first four seasons as head coach. All the meanwhile, the Tigers were stockpiling their roster with more elite talent as they continued to gain momentum on the recruiting trail, luring the likes of future NFL players Andre Ellington, DeAndre Hopkins, Sammy Watkins, Martavis Bryant, and Vic Beasley to Clemson.

In 2013, with Boyd now a senior, the Tigers entered the year ranked No. 8 nationally and would rise to as high as No. 3 before falling to

No. 5 Florida State in the seventh week of the season. After once again climbing to No. 6 in the AP Top 25 thanks to four consecutive double-digit blowout victories, Clemson's regular season ended on a sour note with a 31–17 loss to South Carolina in the Battle for the Palmetto State.

That, however, wouldn't stop the Tigers from proving themselves one game later. With a 40–35 victory over Ohio State and Meyer in the Orange Bowl, Clemson cemented its status as one of college football's top modern programs, clinching a top-10 finish for the school for the first time since the end of the 1991 campaign.

"It means we're one step closer to our goal," Swinney said of the significance of the win. "Which is to be the best in the country."

Weeks later, a four-star quarterback from Gainesville, Georgia, named Deshaun Watson arrived at Clemson as an early enrollee and would help take the Tigers to heights they had never seen.

After a 10–3 season in 2014, Clemson entered 2015 ranked No. 12 nationally before riding an undefeated run through the middle of November to a No. 1 ranking for the first time since the school's lone national championship in 1981. With a win over North Carolina in the ACC Championship Game, the top-ranked Tigers clinched a spot in the second-ever College Football Playoff and would advance to the national title following a 37–17 victory over Oklahoma in the Orange Bowl semifinal.

Clemson's bid for its first national title in 34 years, however, would fall short and for Swinney, it would be to a familiar foe. With a 45–40 win over the Tigers in the College Football Playoff Championship Game, Alabama won its 16th national title in program history.

"Right now all of our hearts are broken. We really wanted, obviously, to win this game and to be 15–0," Swinney said afterward. "This program doesn't take a back seat to anybody. We can play with anybody. We can beat anybody, and that's a fact."

With the bulk of its roster returning a year later, Clemson entered 2016 with no shortage of expectations as the nation's preseason No. 2 team. After two weeks, however, the Tigers would tumble to No. 5 thanks to close calls against Auburn and Troy and would spend much of the campaign seemingly underperforming, despite starting the season on a nine-game winning streak.

On November 12, Pitt handed No. 3 Clemson its first regular season loss in nearly two calendar years, but the Tigers only fell to No. 5 and remained in control of their ACC destiny. The defeat also seemed to bring out the best in the Tigers, who closed the regular season with blowout victories over Wake Forest and South Carolina before punching their ticket to the playoff as the No. 2 seed with a win over Virginia Tech in the ACC title game.

After beating the Buckeyes soundly in the Fiesta Bowl, No. 2 Clemson was set for a rematch with the No. 1 Crimson Tide in the national title game. And for the first half, their second meeting appeared to be headed for a similar result to their first, with Alabama jumping out to a 14–0 halftime lead.

After the Tigers cut the Crimson Tide's advantage to three on a Watson-to-Hunter Renfrow 24-yard touchdown pass in the middle of the third quarter, Alabama took a 24–14 lead into the fourth following a 68-yard score by tight end O.J. Howard.

Watson, however, would find wideout Mike Williams for a touchdown one minute into the fourth quarter and the Tigers then took the lead with 4:38 left on the clock after a Wayne Gallman one-yard touchdown run. Freshman quarterback Jalen Hurts then regained the lead for the Tide with a 30-yard run, leaving Clemson trailing by three points with just more than two minutes remaining in the game.

What would follow would be one of the most memorable drives in college football history. In nine plays, Watson—a two-time Heisman Trophy finalist—drove the Tigers 68 yards, finding Renfrow—who, like Swinney, was once a walk-on wide receiver—for a two-yard completion in the end zone with one second remaining in the game.

"To me, that moment, that epitomizes what our program is all about," Swinney said after the game. "You've got the five-star quarterback throwing the game-winning touchdown to the walk-on wideout, and that's the epitome of our team. It doesn't matter if you're the five-star guy or the walk-on, best player plays. You earn it. There's no entitlement in our program. You earn it. Period."

The play would cap one of the most storied careers of any quarterback in college football history for Watson and give Clemson its first national championship in 35 years. It would also make Swinney arguably the hottest current coach in all of college football, given what the Tigers have accomplished and continue to build on the recruiting trail under his watch.

"I can't tell you how humbled I am, blessed, and so thankful to be a part of helping get Clemson back on top this moment. 35 years, doing something that a lot of people didn't think we could do. I'm so thankful for that opportunity," Swinney said. "I'm excited about continuing to help Clemson be the best. I truly am. We're going to work our tails off. As I said out there earlier, one thing about our team is once we've done something once, we'll do it again."

But while Swinney may currently own bragging rights over Meyer—and the rest of the college football world—he still has a long way to go to catch up to the Ohio State head coach. At this point, his head coaching career has lasted just about half as long as Meyer's has and it's worth noting that Meyer won not just one, but two national titles in his first eight seasons as a head coach.

In addition to his three national championships, Meyer holds an .851–.761 advantage over Swinney when it comes to their respective winning percentages as well.

Make no mistake: Swinney is one of the best—if not *the* best—active coaches in college football today. In terms of his overall legacy, he could even be the next Urban Meyer.

Just more than eight years into his head coaching career, he's off to a strong start. But he still has some catching up to do before moving from a current great into an all-time great, as Meyer has.

Urban Meyer vs. Pete Carroll

Technically, Urban Meyer and Pete Carroll were never actually rivals. In fact, at no point in their respective careers—either as head coaches or assistants—have the two coaches ever stood on opposing sidelines. The closest the two ever came to doing so came when Carroll accepted the head coaching job at USC in the same year that Meyer left Notre Dame for Bowling Green.

But if ever there was a challenger to Meyer's "Coach of the 2000s" crown, it was Carroll, whose Trojans teams compiled a mini dynasty in the first half of the decade. Having each spent time under the tutelage of Lou Holtz and Earle Bruce, the two could be considered kindred spirits of sorts, with Meyer even admitting he's adopted Carroll's philosophy when it comes to redshirting players.

"When [players] are here, we don't say, 'We are going to save you and let you mature a little bit.' That used to be a big deal in college football,"

Meyer said in 2015. "Pete Carroll, I stole that from him. One day, I was listening to him talk at USC back in 2006, and he says, 'We don't red-shirt guys here.' I thought, how cool is that? Go out and recruit guys that go play. Because kids want to play."

Having each accepted his first head coaching job in 2001, the two coaches spent their first nine years standing on a college sideline on nearly identical trajectories. From 2001 to 2009, Carroll amassed a 97–17 record, while Meyer's mark stood at 96–18.

And although they never crossed paths—thanks in large part due to large portions of Carroll's having been spent in the NFL—it's tough to pinpoint Meyer's place in college football history without comparing it to the only other head coach as synonymous with the 2000s as he is.

Unlike Stoops and Swinney, Carroll didn't get his start in coaching at a major college football program. A native of San Francisco, California, Carroll played football, basketball, and baseball at Larkspur Redwood High School, but was too small to earn a Division I scholarship.

Instead, Carroll enrolled at College of Marin, a junior college, where he played defensive back. After two seasons at Marin, Carroll transferred to the University of the Pacific, which possessed a Division I-A football program at the time. In his two seasons playing safety for the Tigers, Carroll earned All–Pacific Coast Athletic Conference honors.

After failing to catch on in the World Football League and a short stint as a roofing salesman, Carroll returned to Pacific and joined head coach Chester Caddas' staff as a graduate assistant, working with the defensive backs and wide receivers.

Carroll would hold the position for four years, with the Tigers accumulating a 20–16 record over that span. In 1977, he joined Holtz's first staff at the University of Arkansas in a similar role.

In Carroll's lone season in Fayetville, the Razorbacks amassed an 11–1 record, beating No. 2 Oklahoma in the Orange Bowl to finish the

1977 campaign ranked No. 3 in the nation. The following off-season, Bruce—then the head coach at Iowa State—hired Carroll to be his secondary coordinator, a role he would keep as he followed his boss to Ohio State a year later. The Buckeyes enjoyed an 11–0 regular season in Bruce's first season in Columbus and had a chance to win the national title, but fell to USC by a score of 17–16 in the Rose Bowl.

In 1980, Carroll's ascent up the coaching ranks continued, as North Carolina State head coach Monte Kiffin—Arkansas' defensive coordinator during Carroll's lone season with the Razorbacks—hired him to be the Wolfpack's defensive coordinator. After Kiffin left Raleigh to pursue opportunities in the NFL after just three seasons, Carroll returned to his alma mater, joining Bob Cope's Pacific staff as an assistant head coach and offensive coordinator.

Like so many of his previous stints, Carroll's return to the Tigers would only last for a single season. In 1984, he made his first jump to the NFL, joining Kay Stephenson's Buffalo Bills staff as a defensive backs coach. It wouldn't take long for Carroll to be introduced to the realities of professional football, as the Bills endured a 2–14 campaign in his first season in Buffalo.

Carroll, however, would find stability in the coming years, as he joined Bud Grant's Minnesota Vikings staff as a defensive backs coach. Carroll would spend five seasons in Minnesota and was a part of four winning seasons and three playoff appearances. It was during this time that Carroll became a true riser in the coaching ranks and garnered consideration for the head coaching vacancy at Stanford in 1989 that was ultimately filled by Dennis Green.

His next promotion would come just a year later, as New York Jets head coach Bruce Coslet hired Carroll to be his defensive coordinator prior to the 1990 season.

With an 8–8 record, the Jets made the 1991 playoffs, but failed to amass a winning record in any of Carroll's five seasons as Coslet's defensive coordinator. Nonetheless, the franchise opted to promote Carroll to head coach after firing Coslet following the 1993 campaign.

The Jets got off to a 4–3 start in Carroll's first season as a head coach, but would finish the year with a 6–10 mark after losing their final five contests. New York proceeded to fire Carroll after just one year.

Carroll would catch on with the defending Super Bowl–champion San Francisco 49ers, serving as George Seifert's defensive coordinator. The New England Patriots then hired him to replace Bill Parcells in 1997, after Carroll's 49ers defenses ranked in the top five in each of his two seasons in San Francisco.

Carroll got off to a strong start in his return to the head coaching ranks, with the Patriots amassing a 10–6 record and winning the AFC East division title. The team would make the playoffs again the following year with a 9–7 record, but fell to 8–8 in 1999.

"A lot of things were going on that made it difficult for him to stay, some of which were out of his control," Patriots owner Kraft said, per the New York *Daily News*. "And it began with following a legend."

Having twice been fired in the span of six seasons and now in his late 40s, Carroll's future as a head coach was cloudy. Rather than return somewhere as a defensive coordinator—a position he had found plenty of success at—he'd sit out the 2000 season to serve as a consultant for both pro and college teams.

In 2001, however, Carroll would get his third shot as a head coach—albeit after the University of Southern California swung and missed in luring Mike Bellotti, Dennis Erickson, and Mike Riley to Los Angeles. As he accepted the position following an embarrassing and public coaching search, Carroll had no illusions about the reality of the situation.

"I've been an unpopular choice in the past," Carroll said, per the *Los Angeles Times*. "What it is, it's a challenge."

It would also turn out to be the role of a lifetime and arguably the defining stint of Carroll's coaching career as he helped resurrect a once-proud program.

While his 6–6 debut in 2001 may have provided more of the same for a Trojans team that had spent the better part of the previous decade floundering in mediocrity, Carroll's enthusiastic and infectious personality quickly became a big hit in the laid-back Los Angeles market. It would prove fruitful on the recruiting trail as well, as in his first full recruiting cycle at USC, Carroll netted a top-10 class.

It wouldn't take long for the on-field results to follow.

Behind the play of Heisman Trophy–winning quarterback Carson Palmer, the Trojans enjoyed a 10–2 regular season in 2002, winning USC's first conference title since 1995. In the Orange Bowl against Iowa, USC cemented its status as one of the nation's top teams, beating the Hawkeyes 38–17 before finishing No. 4 in the final AP Top 25 and Coaches Poll.

Despite losing the likes of Palmer and star safety Troy Polamalu to the NFL, the Trojans would only improve in the coming year, as redshirt quarterback Matt Leinart and a roster infused with a top-five nationally ranked recruiting class led USC to an 11–1 regular season record and a second straight Pac-12 title.

Its lone loss of the year coming in triple overtime against Cal, USC would finish the regular season ranked No. 2 in the AP Top 25, but still trailed both Oklahoma and LSU in the final BCS standings. As a result, the Trojans found themselves on the outside looking in when it came to the BCS national title game Sugar Bowl. But after USC beat No. 4 Michigan in convincing fashion in the Rose Bowl and LSU knocked off the top-ranked Sooners, the Trojans were voted the

Associated Press national champions, marking the only split national title of the BCS era.

For USC, it marked the program's first claimed national title in 25 years. It wouldn't take long for the Trojans to add their next—and this time, there wouldn't be any disputing it.

Returning Leinart at quarterback, an emerging star in Reggie Bush at running back, and seven starters on defense, USC entered the 2004 campaign as the preseason No. 1 team. What would follow would be one of the most dominant seasons in college football history, as the Trojans averaged 38.2 points per game en route to Leinart winning the Heisman Trophy and a 12–0 regular season record.

USC saved its best for last, blowing out undefeated Oklahoma 55–19 in the Orange Bowl BCS title game, becoming just the second team in college football to go wire-to-wire as the nation's No. 1 team through the entirety of a season.

Even with Auburn compiling an undefeated season of its own, the Trojans were the undisputed national champion in both the BCS and AP poll.

"I think we proved tonight that we are the No. 1 team in the country without a doubt," Leinart said, per the AP.

In the weeks following USC's national title-game victory, Leinart would surprise many by opting to forgo the NFL draft in order to return to Los Angeles for his senior season. Returning eight starters on offense and five on defense, the two-time defending national champions appeared poised for a threepeat.

And by the end of the 2005 regular season, Carroll seemed to have reached the peak of his powers in L.A.

Compiling a second straight undefeated regular season, the Trojans remained the nation's top-ranked team for nearly two full calendar years and carried a 34-game winning streak into the Rose Bowl.

Leinart would miss out on repeating as the Heisman Trophy winner, having been beaten out by his teammate, Bush, marking the third time in four years one of Carroll's players won college football's most prestigious individual award.

As it prepared to tangle with No. 2 Texas in Pasadena, a third straight national championship for Carroll and USC felt like more of formality than anything else. Vince Young and the Longhorns, however, had other ideas.

In one of the greatest college football games ever played, which featured 15 players who would be picked in the 2006 NFL draft, Texas topped the Trojans 41–38 when Young, the Longhorns' star quarterback, scored on an eight-yard run with 19 seconds remaining in the game. Over the course of the next three seasons, Carroll's USC teams would compile a 34–5 record, win three more Pac-12 titles, and win three Rose Bowls, but would never again play for the BCS national title.

Following the 2009 season, which saw the Trojans compile a 9–4 record and a victory in the Emerald Bowl, Carroll returned to the NFL, accepting the Seattle Seahawks head coach position. In his first seven seasons in Seattle, Carroll has found significantly more success in the pros than he did during his previous stints, compiling a 70–41–1 record, four division titles, and a victory in Super Bowl XLVIII.

Yet despite his recent run, no figure is more synonymous with the modern USC program—or 2000s college football, for that matter—than Carroll, for reasons both good and bad.

In 2010, following a four-year investigation into improper benefits received by players, including Bush, the NCAA cited the USC athletic department for a lack of institutional control. As a result, the Trojans were forced to vacate 14 wins from the 2004 and 2005 seasons, including USC's BCS championship victory over Oklahoma in the 2005 Orange Bowl, and Bush was forced to forfeit his Heisman Trophy. The football program was also placed on a two-year postseason ban and stripped of 30 scholarships over a three-year span.

In the seven seasons since Carroll's departure, the Trojans have recorded a combined 62–30 record under the direction of three separate full-time head coaches.

But even with all he left behind, it's hard not to remember Carroll for his run in the mid-2000s and think what could have been had he and Meyer ever crossed paths.

Counting Carroll's victories, the two coaches possess nearly identical résumés, with Meyer possessing a winning percentage of .851 and Carroll posting a success rate of .836 in his nine seasons at the helm in L.A. Both coaches won three national titles and lay claim to impressive bowl records, including a 10–2 mark for Meyer and a 7–2 tally for Carroll.

Over the course of his career, Meyer has won five conference championships, while Carroll won seven. Each has been one of the best when it's come to putting players in the pros as well, with Meyer having produced 61 draft picks as of the 2016 NFL draft—the exact same number of players USC had selected from 2002 to 2010.

But for all the similarities between the two head coaches, several dissimilarities exist as well. Meyer has spent the entirety of his coaching career at the college level, while Carroll has seamlessly shifted between the preps and pros.

Would Meyer ever consider one day making the jump to the NFL, à la Carroll?

"I don't think so," Meyer said in 2009, a sentiment he would echo in 2015.

It's also worth noting that while a large portion of Carroll's résumé has been officially vacated in the record books, Meyer's programs have never been found guilty of—or even investigated for—an NCAA violation. For that reason alone, Meyer's legacy at the college level will likely be remembered more fondly.

But even if, for now, it remains a dream matchup only possible in video games, make no mistake; a meeting between Meyer and Carroll—two of the most dominant coaches ever to do it over the course of a decade—would be welcomed with open arms.

★ ★ ★

Urban Meyer vs. Steve Spurrier

For all he accomplished in his six seasons in Gainesville—a 65–15 record, two national championships, and two SEC titles highlight heights the program had never previously seen—Urban Meyer will never be considered the most prominent coach in the history of Florida football.

That's because no figure in Gators football will ever be more synonymous with Meyer's former employer than Steve Spurrier.

In fact, Meyer may never have wound up in Gainesville in the first place if not for all Spurrier accomplished over the course of his 12 seasons standing on the sideline of "the Swamp." Factor in his status as one of the greatest players in Florida football history as well, and it's not a stretch to say that Spurrier is responsible for putting the Gators on the map.

"I don't think Urban Meyer is coaching at the University of Florida if we didn't have the type of program Steve Spurrier created," Florida athletic director Jeremy Foley said in 2009, per the *Orlando Sentinel*.

For many reasons out of his own control, Meyer's own career in Gainesville was inevitably intertwined and consistently compared with Spurrier's, who served as an SEC East rival at South Carolina.

But in order to truly understand why Meyer and Spurrier's respective careers will always be linked, you must first learn how the "Head Ball Coach" carved his own unique corner in college football and Florida history.

The son of a minister, Spurrier was born in Miami, Florida, but raised in Tennessee, and earned a reputation as a standout athlete from an early age. At Science Hill High School, in Johnson City, Tenn., Spurrier starred as a three-sport athlete, with most—including his father—believing that either baseball or basketball was his best sport.

But while Spurrier didn't necessarily disagree with that notion, it was football that served as his first love. As two-year starter at quarterback in head coach Kermit Tipton's open-style passing offense, Spurrier earned All-America honors in his senior year.

After receiving scholarship offers from some of the nation's top programs, including Alabama, Georgia, Mississippi, and North Carolina, Spurrier settled on the University of Florida, citing "the passing, the SEC, the weather, and coach Ray Graves" as reasons why in Bill Chastian's 2002 book *The Steve Spurrier Story: From Heisman to Head Ball Coach.*

After sitting out the 1963 season as a freshman, Spurrier alternated in and out of the Gators' starting lineup with senior Tommy Shannon in 1964, earning the SEC's Sophomore of the Year Award. The following year, Spurrier had Florida's starting quarterback job all to himself and in 1966, he led the Gators to a 9–2 record—arguably their best season in program history at that point.

With a penchant for leading dramatic comebacks that led John Logue of the *Atlanta Journal Constitution* to write, "blindfolded, with his back to the wall, with his hands tied behind him, Steve Spurrier would be a two-point favorite at his own execution," Spurrier earned first-team All-America honors as a senior and won the first Heisman Trophy in program history—doing so by what was the largest margin in the history of the award at the time.

Spurrier finished his Gators career as the most accomplished player in the history of the program, completing 56.6 percent of his pass attempts for 4,848 yards and 36 touchdowns in three years.

With one scouting report, according to the *Gainesville Sun*, describing him as having "the arm of Sammy Baugh, the poise of Johnny Unitas, the leadership of Norm Van Brocklin, and the quickness of Joe Namath," the San Francisco 49ers traded up to select Spurrier with the No. 3 overall pick of the 1967 NFL draft.

Starting his career sitting behind All-Pro John Brodie, Spurrier never lived up to the hype as a pro prospect. Over the course of 10 seasons, he started 38 games, the highlights of his career including a 6–2–1 record in nine games as a starter in 1972 and a 240-yard, three-touchdown performance in a 24–23 comeback victory over the Los Angeles Rams in 1975. He spent his final season in the NFL with the Tampa Bay Buccaneers, starting 12 games throughout the expansion team's unceremonious run to an 0–14 record.

After being released by the Bucs and failing to catch on with the Denver Broncos or Miami Dolphins, Spurrier retired, having totaled 6,878 yards, 40 touchdowns, 60 interceptions and 230 punts for a 38.3-yard average.

Spurrier spent the 1977 season away from football, but joined Doug Dickey's Florida staff as a quarterback and receivers coach a year later, as the Gators head coach looked to replace his team's run-heavy offensive approach with a pro-style attack. After a 4–7 season, however, Dickey was fired and replaced by Clemson coach Charley Pell, who opted not to retain Spurrier or any of his predecessor's staff.

After debating whether or not he wanted to remain in coaching, Spurrier joined Pepper Rodgers' Georgia Tech staff as a quarterbacks coach. Much like his previous stint in Gainesville, however, Spurrier would again be one-and-done, as Rodgers was fired following a 4–6–1 season.

Having not been retained by incoming Yellow Jackets coach Bill Curry, Spurrier was then hired by Duke head coach Red Wilson to serve as the Blue Devils' offensive coordinator. Spurrier would spend three seasons in Durham, implementing a pass-heavy attack that led to quarterback Ben Bennett setting an NCAA record for career passing yards.

Suddenly an up-and-comer in the coaching ranks, the 37-year-old Spurrier would parlay his success at Duke into his first head coaching job, taking over as the head coach of the USFL's Tampa Bay Bandits. With a wide-open offense branded "BanditBall" that rivaled the cross-town Bucs in terms of popularity, Spurrier led the Bandits to a 35–21 record before the USFL dissolved after three seasons.

With the USFL having played its games in the spring, Spurrier was left without a job entering the 1986 campaign. He would interview for the LSU opening at the end of the year, but ultimately returned to Duke, this time as the head coach and offensive coordinator.

It was during his second stint in Durham that Spurrier developed a reputation for winning—and enhancing—rivalry games. From 1987 to '89, he recorded a 3–0 record against North Carolina, including a 41–0 win over the Tar Heels that clinched the Blue Devils' first ACC title since 1962. After the game, Spurrier urged his team to take a photo in front of the Kenan Memorial Stadium scoreboard, which irritated UNC fans.

The Tar Heels, however, wouldn't get the opportunity to seek revenge. After twice being named the ACC's Coach of the Year, Florida hired Spurrier to replace head coach Galen Hall at the end of the 1989 campaign.

With the Gators having floundered in mediocrity for the better part of the previous decade, Spurrier set out to restore tradition to his alma mater. At his introductory press conference, Spurrier cited bringing back the Gators' blue jersey tops, natural grass at Florida Field, and restoring their rivalry with Miami as objectives to help accomplish that.

Most importantly, he set out to win championships—something Florida couldn't claim to have done in program history.

It wouldn't take long for Spurrier to change that.

In Spurrier's first season back in Gainesville, he would lead the Gators, who were ineligible for postseason play due to NCAA violations committed under Hall, to a 9–2 record. A year later, Florida would win 10 games for the first time in program history and the school's first SEC championship.

Dubbed the "Fun 'N Gun," Spurrier's wide-open offense was an instant success. From 1991 to '96, the Gators compiled a 64–12–1 record, winning the program's first five SEC championships along the way.

That alone would have been good enough to make Spurrier's run the most successful in Florida history, but in 1996, he took the Gators to heights the program had never seen. Behind a Heisman Trophy–winning season from quarterback Danny Wuerffel—the second in school history, in addition to Spurrier's—Florida clinched its first national championship with a convincing 52–20 win over rival Florida State in the Sugar Bowl.

With his signature visor and a habit of poking fun SEC rivals such as Tennessee, Spurrier had become the most prominent player and now coach in Florida history. After his national championship season in Gainesville, he'd spend five more seasons coaching the Gators, compiling a career record of 122–27–1.

In 2002, he took his first head coaching job in the NFL when the Washington Redskins hired him to replace Marty Schottenheimer.

His Fun N' Gun approach, however, didn't translate well to the pros, as Washington's 7–9 record in 2002 marked the franchise's first losing season in seven years.

After a 5–11 campaign in 2003, Redskins owner Dan Snyder pulled the plug on the Spurrier experiment.

"When I left Florida after 12 years, I thought I was going to coach in the NFL five or six years and retire to the beach, and play golf a bunch, and travel around, this, that and the other," Spurrier would later say. "But that was a bad plan. It was. Later you found out that was not a real good idea. But that's the way I was thinking back then."

Spurrier would sit out the 2004 campaign and when Florida fired his successor, Ron Zook, midway through the season, many connected him to his alma mater and former employer. Ultimately, the Gators opted to hire Meyer instead.

Spurrier wouldn't be far away, however, as he replaced Lou Holtz at the University of South Carolina, which like Florida is a member of the SEC East. The Gamecocks would beat the Gators 30–22 in the first meeting between Meyer and Spurrier, but failed to keep pace with Florida in the long run.

As Meyer led the Gators to their second and third national championships in program history, Spurrier managed just one division title in 10 years in Columbia, tallying an 86–49 overall record, retiring six games into a 2–4 start to the 2015 campaign.

Adding another win over Meyer in 2010—his first victory in Gainesville as an opposing coach—Spurrier netted a 2–4 career record in head-to-head matchups against the only other coach to lead his alma mater to the promised land.

While Spurrier holds an edge over Meyer in terms of longevity, Meyer's three national titles and career .851 winning percentage tell the story of a more consistent coach. The two coaches' respective résumés, however, are much more comparable when only taking into account their years at Florida.

While Meyer amassed an .813 winning percentage in his six seasons in Gainesville, Spurrier produced an even more impressive .817 mark— and did so in twice as many seasons. Meyer holds the edge in national championships, but Spurrier won four more SEC titles and as Foley mentioned, was the first head coach to put Florida on the map.

Ultimately, when considering his longevity and playing career, it's understandable why Florida fans seem to remember Spurrier more fondly than they do Meyer, even though the latter's peak accounted for arguably the highest point in program history.

Between the sustained success Meyer found at Bowling Green, Utah, Florida, and now Ohio State, there's no doubting which coach possesses a higher place in the hierarchy of college football's all-time great coaches.

But when it comes to just the Gators, there's also no doubting which coach lays claim to the title of "Mr. Florida Football."

★   ★   ★

Urban Meyer vs. Lane Kiffin

Make no mistake about it—Lane Kiffin is hardly in the same class of head coach as Urban Meyer when it comes to the two coaches' respective career résumés.

While Meyer has spent his career climbing the coaching mountain and maintaining his status as one of college football's premier coaches, Kiffin has seen a once-promising career derailed and since rebooted.

Yet it's impossible to tell the full story of Meyer's history in coaching rivalries without mentioning the first public feud of his to gain national notoriety. Whenever one thinks of the great rivalries in Meyer's career, Kiffin's name—despite not carrying the same weight of a Saban or Jim Harbaugh—often tops the list.

How did the Meyer–Kiffin rivalry come to be, no less before Kiffin had ever even coached in a college game? We'll get there in a minute.

But first, a little background on the head coach who first felt the wrath of an agitated Meyer.

If ever there was a coaching prodigy born into the profession, it was Lane Kiffin. The son of onetime North Carolina State head coach and longtime NFL defensive coordinator Monte Kiffin, Lane spent his childhood following his father across the country from Nebraska to Arkansas, Raleigh, Green Bay, and Buffalo, before starring as the quarterback at Bloomington Jefferson High School in Minnesota, where his father was serving as the Vikings' defensive coordinator.

After high school, Kiffin would head to Fresno State, where he served as a backup quarterback for three seasons before joining the Bulldogs staff as a student assistant, working alongside quarterbacks coach Jeff Tedford.

In 1999, Kiffin ventured to Colorado State as a graduate assistant under head coach Sonny Lubick, who had also been Meyer's boss during his final three seasons in Fort Collins. After one season with the Rams, Kiffin took his first job in the NFL, joining Tom Coughlin's Jacksonville Jaguars staff as an offensive quality control coach.

He wouldn't have to wait long for his next big opportunity.

In 2001, Pete Carroll—who had worked alongside Monte Kiffin at Arkansas and North Carolina State—hired Lane to be the tight ends coach on his first staff at USC. The return to Southern California would accelerate the career trajectory of the 26-year-old Kiffin, who took over coaching the Trojans' wide receivers in 2002.

After spending three seasons developing the likes of Mike Williams, Keary Colbert, Steve Smith, and Dwayne Jarrett as USC won back-to-back national titles, Kiffin was promoted to offensive coordinator in 2005 following the departure of Norm Chow.

Barely 30 years old, Kiffin was now the offensive coordinator at the country's premier program and one of the hottest young coaches in all of college football. He'd spend two seasons with the Trojans, directing the nation's No. 2 offense in 2005 and No. 18 unit in 2006 before being hired as the head coach of the Oakland Raiders in 2007.

His first foray as a head coach, however, would be short-lived.

Following a 4–12 debut season in 2007, reports circulated that Raiders owner Al Davis had attempted to force the 32-year-old Kiffin to resign. Nevertheless, he would return for the 2008 campaign, but was fired four games into the season following a 1–3 start.

Given the perceived dysfunction of the Raiders franchise, Kiffin's coaching future remained bright.

In 2009, Tennessee hired Kiffin to replace longtime head coach Phillip Fulmer. It was at Kiffin's introductory press conference in Knoxville that his feud with Meyer—who was coming off his second national title in three seasons at the time—began.

"I'm really looking forward to embracing some of the great traditions at the University of Tennessee," Kiffin said. "Singing 'Rocky Top' all night long after we beat Florida next year. It's going to be a blast, okay? So get ready."

While Kiffin's comments could have initially been construed as an attempt to galvanize his fan base while displaying confidence against an SEC rival, it became clear just two months later that the 33-year-old head coach was intentionally targeting the biggest dog in the yard.

At a signing-day celebration in front of a crowd of boosters, Kiffin spoke of his first Volunteers recruiting class, which according to 247Sports .com ranked No. 8 nationally—one spot behind No. 7 Florida. When it came time to discuss four-star wideout and former Gators commit Nu'keese Richardson, Kiffin again took aim at Meyer, accusing the Florida head coach of having committed NCAA recruiting violations.

"I'm going to turn Florida in right here in front of you," Kiffin told the crowd. "As Nu'Keese was here on campus, his phone keeps ringing.

It may be low-key, but Meyer's rivalry with Lane Kiffin is one of the most important of his coaching career.

And so one of our coaches is sitting in a meeting with him and he says, 'Who's that?' and he looks at the phone and it says 'Urban Meyer.' Just so you know, when a recruit is on another campus, you can't call a recruit on another campus.

"I love the fact that Urban Meyer had to cheat and still didn't get him."

As it turned out, Meyer had not committed a violation. In fact, shortly thereafter, Kiffin was the one forced to issue a public apology following a reprimand from the SEC for violating a conference policy regarding public criticism of other member institutions, their staffs, or players.

"His allegations are inappropriate, out of line and, most importantly, totally false," Florida athletic director Jeremy Foley said in the statement. "It is completely unfair to Urban Meyer, our coaching staff, our football program, and our institution."

Kiffin's comments also drew the ire of the Gators players, who plastered his quotes all throughout the Florida facility as early as spring football. When asked on ESPN's *First Take* about having needled college football's premier program, Kiffin replied, "I think it's a neat thing that Tennessee's logo is all over Florida's locker room."

As for Kiffin's guarantee that Tennessee would top the defending national champions later that season, that too, would prove unfounded. In the 2009 SEC opener for both teams, the top-ranked Gators topped the Volunteers—who would finish the season with a 7–6 record—23–13.

After the game, Kiffin would stop short of claiming a moral victory. He would, however, insist that his display of confidence directed at Florida nearly a year prior was all a part of his plan.

"It took all the pressure off the players," he said of the media and fan focus on his verbal jabs at Florida and coach Urban Meyer. "We played the No. 1 team in the nation, with no pressure on [Tennessee]. It was all on me. We're running out of the tunnel, and all those people are yelling at me, and not one person is yelling at them."

Meyer had done his best to distance himself from a war of words with Kiffin, but following their first matchup, he accused the Volunteers head coach of playing to keep the game close, rather than to win.

"When I saw them start handing the ball off, I didn't feel like they were going after the win," Meyer said of Tennessee's fourth-quarter play-calling.

To which Kiffin responded, "This off-season the commissioner made a big deal of renewing vows in terms of what we say about other teams, other coaches, and other players. Urban feels he doesn't need to follow that. We won't say anything else."

Later that season, Kiffin would take a backhanded jab at Meyer's disciplinary problems in Gainesville and in November 2009, Bleacher Report deemed the Meyer–Kiffin feud the "SEC's premier coaching rivalry." There wouldn't, however, be a second installment. After Carroll left USC to become the head coach of the Seattle Seahawks, Kiffin abruptly departed from Knoxville to replace his former boss as the Trojans head coach.

On the same night as Kiffin's highly publicized parting, Meyer was caught on camera at a Florida basketball game smirking as he received a text. While it could have just been a coincidence, many have speculated—or at least joked—that the clip was Meyer's real-time reaction to Kiffin's ugly exit.

Kiffin would amass a 28–15 career record as the head coach at USC before being fired by the school following a 3–2 start to the 2013 campaign. In 2014, Saban hired Kiffin as his new offensive coordinator, leading Kiffin and Meyer's paths to cross once again in the College Football Playoff semifinal Sugar Bowl later that year.

Asked about rekindling his formerly publicized rivalry with Meyer, Kiffin insisted the two had since patched up their rocky relationship.

"Coach Meyer and myself communicated a few times over texts, phone calls," Kiffin said. "I don't remember the timing of it. And it was, hey, all this kind of crap from before, let's move on. I obviously have great respect for what he's done everywhere he's been and how fast he's gotten this program up to being the top four team in the country."

Meyer would get the best of Kiffin and the Crimson Tide en route to winning the College Football Playoff championship that year, but over the course of three seasons under Saban in Tuscaloosa—including a national championship campaign in 2015—Kiffin appeared to have rehabilitated his image. Following the 2016 season, Florida Atlantic University hired Kiffin as its head coach.

At his introductory press conference with the Owls, Kiffin once again mentioned Meyer. This statement, however, stood in stark contrast to the challenge he had issued eight years prior.

"I'm not concerned about sending a message to the rest of the conference," Kiffin said. "I've sent those messages before, to Coach Meyer at Tennessee when I said we were going to sing Rocky Top all night long in the Swamp. That didn't go over very well. That's taken about 8 to 10 years to get back to buddies with Coach Meyer. We're a lot better now."

Nevertheless, the brief but memorable feud between Meyer and Kiffin will continue to hold its own special place in SEC history.

The 41-year-old Kiffin still has a long way to go to catch Meyer in most—if not all—career accolades. And as he just now begins to restart his trek up the head coaching ranks, he may never get there.

But when it comes to coaches unafraid to bring out the best in Meyer from a rivalry standpoint, Kiffin's name will always be at the top of the list.

★ ★ ★

Urban Meyer vs. Nick Saban

As the calendar prepared to turn from 1989 to 1990, Urban Meyer's professional coaching career was just four years young and already appeared to be stalling. Having spent his previous two seasons as an assistant at Division I Football Championship Subdivision Illinois State, Meyer was desperate to return to the college football's highest level.

In an effort to do so, Meyer tried to go home—emphasis on the word *tried*.

The University of Toledo, which is located less than five miles away from the hospital in which Meyer was born, had just hired a new head football coach in Houston Oilers defensive backs coach Nick Saban. Meyer figured he'd give the new Rockets head coach a call in an effort to persuade him to let him join his staff.

But when Meyer reached the Saban household, Nick wasn't available. His wife, Terry, however, was, leading the then-25-year-old Meyer to deliver his sales pitch to her instead.

Meyer apparently did an impressive job and when Nick got home, Terry did her best to relay Meyer's message.

"I talked to a really interesting guy today, Urban Meyer," Terry told Nick. "I really do think you should talk to him when you hire your staff."

Saban, however, was still so entrenched in his duties with the Oilers as they prepared for a playoff matchup with the Pittsburgh Steelers that he never got around to calling Meyer back.

"I was so kind of caught up and busy in what I was doing, I never really followed up on that," Saban said in 2014.

The two coaches wouldn't cross paths as head coaches for another 18 years, yet their respective legacies will forever be linked. Urban Meyer and Nick Saban are to college football what Tom Brady and Peyton Manning were to the NFL, LeBron James and Steph Curry are to the NBA, and Alexander Ovechkin and Sidney Crosby are to the NHL— the greatest modern rivalry between two figures the sport has ever seen.

Between the two of them, Meyer and Saban have been responsible for 365 career wins, 41 consensus All-Americans, three Heisman Trophy winners, 156 NFL draft picks (as of 2016), nine top-ranked recruiting classes, and eight national championships among four different schools.

Perhaps most notably, Meyer and Saban have squared off four separate times—with three occasions carrying championship implications. Unsurprisingly, the future Hall of Fame head coaches have split their career series against one another, two games to two.

Yet for the similarities in their success, Meyer and Saban have arrived at their respective places in the college football pantheon via dramatically different routes.

Despite not hearing back from Saban at the end of 1989, Meyer would spend the next decade climbing the assistant coaching ranks before ultimately landing his first head coaching job at Toledo's crosstown rival, Bowling Green. Saban, meanwhile, was in the midst of an already nomadic coaching career, which would ultimately land him at one of the most prominent positions in all of college football.

More than three decades before taking over in Tuscaloosa, Saban's coaching career began—thanks in large part to the woman who once attempted to convince him to hire his future rival.

Born in Fairmont, West Virginia, Nick Saban starred as the quarterback Monongah High School, leading the small town school to a state title in 1968. Although he also earned all-state honors in baseball and basketball, it was football that was Saban's best sport.

Yet due in part to his small-town roots and even more so because of his shorter stature—he is now listed as 5'6"—he was lightly recruited coming out of high school.

"Some big school is really missing out if they don't give Nick a chance," his high school coach, Earl Keener, told the *Raleigh Register* of Saban, who amassed a 28–1–1 career record in three seasons as a starter. "That kid has more heart than any I've ever seen in 20 years of coaching. All he knows how to do is beat you."

Only that big-time offer would never come, with Saban instead choosing to join Don James' Kent State program, choosing the Golden Flashes over offers from Miami (Ohio) and the Naval Academy.

After converting to defensive back, Saban would spend three seasons as a starter on a Kent State defense that also featured future Hall of Fame linebacker Jack Lambert. In 1972, the Golden Flashes won their first— and only—conference title in program history, although Saban's senior season and college career was cut short due to a broken leg.

"I was sort of one of those guys that tried to be an overachiever and was a team guy," Saban said of his playing career in 2016. "I had a lot of fun playing. I loved the competition."

With his playing career over, Saban waited for his high school sweetheart, Terry, to finish her college degree from KSU. While doing so, James recruited Saban to join the Golden Flashes staff as a graduate assistant. Saban would hold the post for two seasons before taking over in a full-time role coaching Kent State's linebackers on Dennis Fitzgerald's staff in 1975.

Saban would venture to Syracuse to join Frank Maloney's staff in 1977, before returning home to West Virginia to coach the Mountaineers defensive backs for head coach Frank Cignetti in 1978. After Cignetti was fired following a 5–6 campaign in 1979, Saban caught on as the defensive backs coach at Ohio State under Earle Bruce in 1980, replacing

Pete Carroll, who had just accepted the defensive coordinator position at North Carolina State.

But after a second consecutive 9–3 season in 1981 ended with a close call against Navy in the Liberty Bowl, Bruce opted to fire the bulk of his defensive staff—including Saban, who had become close to defensive coordinator Dennis Fryzel.

"It was a little bit of a crazy deal," Saban told ESPN. "But I look back more on the mistakes that I made rather than blaming somebody else."

At 30 years old, Saban was back on the job market, landing at Navy as a defensive backs coach for a season, before Michigan State head coach George Perles hired him to take over as the Spartans' defensive coordinator in 1983.

Saban would spend five seasons in East Lansing, including a 9–2–1 campaign in 1987 that resulted in Michigan State's first Big Ten championship a decade and first Rose Bowl victory since 1953. After the season, Oilers coach Jerry Glanville hired Saban as his defensive backs coach.

Houston would enjoy three winning seasons and make the playoffs in each year Saban was on staff, before he took over as the head coach at Toledo in 1990. Taking over a Rockets program that had amassed a 26–28 record over the previous five seasons, Saban would lead Toledo to a 9–2 record and a share of the Mid-American Conference championship in his debut season as a head coach.

His stay in the Glass City, however, would be short-lived. After just one season, Saban resigned from the Rockets to become Bill Belichick's defensive coordinator with the Cleveland Browns.

After starting his Browns career with three consecutive losing seasons, Saban oversaw the NFL's top-ranked defense in 1994 as Cleveland compiled an 11–5 regular season record. Before the 1994 campaign had even come to an end, Michigan State had hired Saban to replace his former boss, Perles as the Spartans' new head coach.

"I am committed to staying at Michigan State for as long as it takes to be a championship team," Saban said the day he was hired, per the *Lansing State Journal*.

Taking over a Spartans program hampered by sanctions stemming from recruiting violations committed under Perles, that, however, proved to be easier said than done. From 1995 to 1998, Saban's teams hovered around .500, amassing a combined 25–22–1 record. The highlight during that stretch would come in 1998, when Michigan State knocked off top-ranked Ohio State in the final month of the season.

That would prove to be a promising sign of things to come as the Spartans totaled a 9–2 record in 1999, the most wins for a Michigan State team since Saban's final season as the team's defensive coordinator in 1987. Under Saban, East Lansing also became a breeding ground for NFL talent, with Michigan State putting players such as Mushin Muhammad, Tony Banks, Derrick Mason, Flozell Adams, Robaire Smith, Julian Peterson, and Plaxico Burress in the pros throughout Saban's tenure. From 1996 to 1999, Saban's Spartans faced Notre Dame—where Meyer served as the wide receivers coach—three times, with Michigan State winning all three matchups.

But despite the Spartans seemingly being on a track to success, Saban wouldn't stick around to coach the team in the Citrus Bowl against Florida, instead accepting the head coaching position at Louisiana State University nearly five years to the day after he was first hired in East Lansing.

"I liked the challenge of this football program," Saban said upon his hiring, per the Associated Press. "I think there is great tradition. I think the Southeastern Conference is a very competitive, outstanding football conference. There's a challenge to being part of that conference that kind of intrigued me."

Alabama head coach Nick Saban congratulates Meyer on the Buckeyes' 42–35 win over the Crimson Tide in the College Football Playoff Semifinal. Ohio State entered the game as a nine-point underdog.

Taking over a former football powerhouse that possessed a combined 7–15 record in the previous two seasons, Saban had his work cut out for him.

In his debut season in Baton Rouge, Saban recorded an 8–4 record, including a victory over Georgia Tech in the Peach Bowl to end the season. The following year, the Tigers won their first SEC title since 1988, capping a 10–3 season with a win over Illinois in the Sugar Bowl.

In 2002, LSU fell to 8–5, but on the recruiting trail, Saban was only gaining steam. In 2003, he inked Rivals.com's top-ranked class, which was headlined by a five-star running back named Justin Vincent.

In his freshman season, Vincent rushed for 1,001 yards and 10 touchdowns, leading the Tigers to an 11–1 regular season record. LSU would then punch its ticket to the BCS Championship Game Sugar Bowl by beating No. 5 Georgia 34–13 in the SEC Championship Game.

Despite entering the game as a six-point underdog, the Tigers would go on to beat Oklahoma 21–14 behind 117 yards and a touchdown from Vincent to win LSU's first national title in 45 years.

Based on Saban's postgame comments, you would never have known the historic nature of what he had just accomplished.

"You don't really want to know what I'm thinking," he said, providing the rare insight into his driven mind-set. "Because what I'm thinking is, how are we going to get this done next year? Because this year's accomplishments are next year's expectations."

The following year, the Tigers would fail to live up to that standard, amassing a 9–3 record to bring Saban's career mark at LSU to 48–16 with two conference titles. His reputation as a coaching mercenary would only be enhanced the following off-season, as he accepted the Miami Dolphins' head coaching job.

In his first season as a head coach in the NFL, Saban recorded a 9–7 record, but the following year the Dolphins would tally just a 6–10 mark. As rumors swirled that he would be leaving South Beach for a return to the college ranks with Alabama, Saban insisted he would be back in Miami for the 2007 campaign.

"I guess I have to say it," Saban famously stated on December 21, 2006. "I'm not going to be the Alabama head coach."

On January 3, 2007, Saban resigned from the Dolphins to become Alabama's 27th head coach in program history.

In returning to the SEC, Saban found himself in a position similar to the one he had eight years prior. With the Crimson Tide, Saban was taking over a once-proud program that had since fallen on hard times, compiling a combined 26–24 record under the direction of Mike Shula from 2003 to 2006.

Saban would lead Alabama to its second consecutive 6–6 regular season in 2007, including a memorable 21–14 loss to Louisiana–Monroe in the second-to-last week of the regular season. The Crimson Tide would go on to beat Colorado in the Independence Bowl to close the season before compiling an undefeated regular season record in 2008.

With a chance to play for the BCS National Championship on the line, the top-ranked Crimson Tide headed to Atlanta for Saban's first head-to-head matchup with Meyer. The Florida head coach would ultimately get the best of the man who forgot to return his call nearly two decades prior, as the Gators knocked off Alabama 31–20 en route to winning their third national championship in three seasons.

Saban and the Crimson Tide wouldn't have to wait long to seek their revenge.

Nearly a year after falling to Florida in the conference title game, Alabama would return to Atlanta once again riding an undefeated regular season run, thanks in large part to the play of Heisman Trophy–winning running back Mark Ingram. Once again taking on the Gators with a BCS Championship Game spot on the line, the Crimson Tide would get the best of the defending national champions, beating Florida by a score of 32–13.

A month later, Alabama would beat 37–21 Texas for the 2009 national championship, making Saban the first coach in college football history to win national titles at two different schools.

After the game, Saban was asked if he ever envisioned the sort of success he was now enjoying as a head coach when he was a young boy.

"Well, first of all, when I was a young boy, I didn't even know I wanted to be a coach," Saban said. "I don't think you ever really envision this kind of success. I think that I was probably driven to try to be as good as I could be at whatever it was that I made a commitment to do. I was that way when I was a player, even though I wasn't a very good player. I worked hard to be the best I could be and had a lot of pride in performance."

In 2010, Saban would once again get the best of Meyer in his final season in Gainesville, as Alabama beat Florida 31–6 in the lone regular season matchup between the two coaches. The Crimson Tide would finish the season with a 10–3 record, including a 49–7 blowout victory over Saban's former employer, Michigan State, in the Capital One Bowl.

The following off-season, Alabama signed the nation's top-ranked class, kickstarting a remarkable run of seven consecutive No. 1–ranked classes for the Crimson Tide that has run through 2017. In just a few short seasons in Tuscaloosa, Saban had Alabama hitting on all cylinders off the field and it wouldn't take long for the results to follow on the field.

From 2011 to 2016, Saban has amassed a 76–8 record, never losing more than two games in a single season. The Crimson Tide would win national championships in 2011, 2012, and 2015, making Saban one of just five head coaches to have won five national championships as he now trails only Alabama legend Bear Bryant (six) for the most by a single coach in college football history.

In a decade in Tuscaloosa, Saban has revolutionized recruiting and way programs put players in the pros. In the first three seasons of the College Football Playoff era, Alabama is the only program to have made the playoff all three times.

At this point, you're probably asking yourself that with all Saban has accomplished, how can Meyer keep up? After all, Saban has the Buckeyes head coach beat when it comes to national championships (5), career victories (210), consensus All-Americans (30), Heisman Trophy winners (2; Derrick Henry would win Saban's second at Alabama in 2015), and players put in the pros (95).

Yet it's worth remembering that the defining moment of Meyer's coaching career came with Saban standing on the opposing sideline. After becoming the first-ever No. 4 seed in the inaugural College Football Playoff, Ohio State was "rewarded" with a Sugar Bowl semifinal showdown with top-ranked Alabama.

Down to their third-string quarterback in Cardale Jones, the Buckeyes entered the game as a 7½-point underdog and quickly fell behind 21–6. By now, you already know the rest. Ohio State would go on to beat mighty 'Bama, before knocking off Oregon to capture Meyer's third national championship.

It would make him the second coach in college football history— after Saban—to win national championships at two separate schools.

Saban and Meyer lay claim to arguably the two healthiest college football programs in the country. On National Signing Day 2017, the Crimson Tide signed the nation's top-ranked class, while the No. 2–ranked Buckeyes' haul laid claim to the highest average player rating of any class in modern recruiting history.

When it comes to their respective legacies, Saban's six-season head start as a college head coach will likely always give him a statistical edge—although it is worth noting that Meyer's .851 career winning percentage bests Saban's .774 mark.

More than anything, however, both Saban and Meyer will be remembered for their respective career arcs and defined by their distinctive dominance than they will be for any numbers. At this point, either coach could retire tomorrow and still be considered the greatest coach of the modern era—and arguably, any era for that matter.

But you can't tell the full story of either coach without bringing up the other. And in that regard, it's fitting that Meyer and Saban have played each other evenly in their four head-to-head matchups.

As for their first encounter—or more accurately, missed connection—at the end of 1989, the two rivals look back on it now and both laugh.

"Obviously, that was a huge mistake on my part," Saban said of failing to hire Meyer at Toledo.

"He said he regrets it? Yeah, I'm sure he does," Meyer joked prior to the Sugar Bowl matchup between the two at the end of the 2014 season. "I'm sure he does. I'm sure that's on his mind right now."

Urban Meyer vs. Bret Bielema

While rival coaches like Lane Kiffin may have done their best to poke Urban Meyer throughout his time in the SEC, Meyer found himself being the coach doing the needling upon joining the Big Ten in 2012—albeit unintentionally.

Joining a once-proud conference that had gone an entire decade without winning a national championship, Meyer brought his intense, win-at-all-costs approach from the SEC up north. That started on the recruiting trail, which Meyer has often referred to as the lifeblood of any college football program.

"I just think overall athleticism right now we're a little bit behind. But we're recruiting with that motive," Meyer said of where his new conference stood in comparison with his former league in 2012. "The defensive front seven in that conference, in the SEC, is the difference maker right now. But it's a little bit deeper than that."

In that regard, it didn't take long for Meyer to make his mark.

Despite having been on the job for just more than two months in Columbus, Meyer signed 26 prospects to his 2012 class, which 247Sports ranked as the nation's No. 5 class. With Michigan coming in at No. 6, the Big Ten's next-highest-ranked class came in at No. 31 Nebraska, which was entering just its second season in the league.

Perhaps most notably, of Meyer's first 26 prospects signed at Ohio State, eight had formerly been committed to other programs, including four-star offensive tackle Kyle Dodson, who had previously pledged to spend his college career at Wisconsin.

Which is where Bret Bielema gets involved.

Entering his seventh season as the Badgers' head coach at the time, Bielema had become accustomed to handling conference recruiting a certain way at the time. Meyer's arrival and aggressive approach, however, shook that up and led to the first-year Ohio State head coach's breaking what some had referred to as a "gentlemen's agreement" between Big Ten coaches that they wouldn't target each other's committed prospects on the recruiting trail.

"There's a few things that happened early on that I made people be aware of, that I didn't want to see in this league, that I had seen take place in other leagues," Bielema told reporters at his National Signing Day press conference, after the Badgers had inked the nation's No. 65–ranked class. "Other recruiting tactics, other recruiting practices, that are illegal…I was very upfront, very pointed to the fact—actually reached out to Coach Meyer and shared my thoughts and concerns with him. The situation got rectified."

Meyer, however, had a different version of the events.

"It's nonsense," Meyer said on his call-in radio show of the alleged gentleman's agreement. "First of all, there's no agreement. And then a kid has the right to go to school wherever he wants. If a kid is interested in a school, he has the right to go look at that school—and that will never change."

While it remains unclear whose side of the story was more accurate, it is worth noting that there's nothing illegal as far as the NCAA is concerned about flipping a committed prospect. In fact, it's since become common practice in the Big Ten and was even defended at the time by, of all people, Kiffin.

That, however, wouldn't stop Bielema from becoming a thorn in Meyer's side—in a similar fashion to the way Kiffin did during the former Florida coach's time in Gainesville. Like Kiffin, Bielema didn't—and probably will never—have the career accolades that could measure up to Meyer's, not that that would ever stop him from being at the center of a battle.

A former walk-on at Iowa who worked his way into becoming a starting defensive lineman, Bielema has always seemed to carry a chip on his shoulder. After going undrafted at the end of his Hawkeyes career, he spent a short stint with the Milwaukee Mustangs in the Arena Football League before beginning his coaching career under Hayden Fry at Iowa in 1994.

In 1996, Bielema was promoted to the Hawkeyes' linebackers coach and he would spend six seasons in the position before Kansas State head coach Bill Snyder hired him as his co–defensive coordinator in 2002. After directing the Wildcats defense to a No. 1 national ranking in his first season in Manhattan and another top-10 finish in his second, Bielema was hired by Wisconsin head coach Barry Alvarez to run the Badgers defense in 2004 and also serve as the program's head coach in waiting.

Taking over a unit that ranked No. 50 nationally the previously year, Bielema helped overhaul Wisconsin's defense, with the Badgers finishing the 2004 campaign ranked No. 6 in the country in total defense. The ensuing off-season, Alvarez announced he would retire at the end of the 2005 season and hand the reins of the program over to Bielema in 2006.

It wouldn't take long for the new head man in Madison to find success.

In his first season as a head coach, Bielema led Wisconsin to a 12–1 record, including a win over Arkansas in the Citrus Bowl to close the season. The Badgers would finish the year ranked No. 5 in the Coaches Poll and No. 7 in the AP, making the then-36-year-old Bielema one of the most promising young head coaches in college football.

Wisconsin would sandwich another pair of top-25 finishes around a 7–6 season in 2008 and in 2010, the Badgers would win what would be the first of three Big Ten championships, including the first two of the league's conference championship game era. The height of his time as Wisconsin's head coach came in 2010, when a defense featuring future NFL superstar J.J. Watt helped lead the Badgers to their second top-10 finish since 1999. The following year, a graduate transfer quarterback named Russell Wilson helped carry Wisconsin to an 11–2 record before losing to Oregon in the Rose Bowl.

Yet Bielema's success on the field never carried over to the recruiting trail, which is perhaps why Meyer's aggressive approach appeared to irk him as much as it did. From 2006 to 2012, none of Bielema's recruiting classes in Madison ever ranked higher than No. 33 nationally and his 2012 haul—on the heels of back-to-back Big Ten championships and NFL draft success—was the least highly touted of the bunch.

Thus began the brief war of words between Meyer and Bielema, which each downplayed when asked about it that summer at Big Ten media days.

"We have a very, very good relationship," Meyer said of Bielema. "I think you'd have to ask coach, but we get along fine. We had a conversation about it at the Big Ten meetings, I believe it was in February. A lot of the things that were reported weren't said. We stand by exactly the way how we do things."

"Urban coming [to the Big Ten as] a coach that's won national championships brings value to our league and his reputation is outstanding," Bielema said, while also insisting it was never the recruitment of committed players that bothered him.

Nevertheless, the November 17 meeting between Ohio State and Wisconsin remained one of the most highly anticipated matchups of the Big Ten schedule that season. And when it arrived in the second-to-last week of the 2012 campaign, the stakes were only enhanced with the Buckeyes riding a 10–0 record and the Badgers having already clinched a Big Ten title-game berth as a result of OSU's postseason ban.

Meyer's first meeting with Bielema in Madison lived up to the hype, as the Buckeyes survived an overtime scare in Camp Randall to keep their undefeated season alive with a 21–14 win over Wisconsin. A week later, Ohio State would clinch an undefeated regular season record with a win over Michigan, but the Badgers had emerged as a worthy secondary rival for the Buckeyes—thanks in large part to the brief feud between the programs' two head coaches.

Much like with Kiffin, however, it would be short-lived. Three weeks after losing to Meyer in their first matchup, Bielema, who once asserted to the *Sporting News* that "we at the Big Ten don't want to be like the SEC in any way, shape or form," left Wisconsin to become the head coach at Arkansas.

Less than a year later, as the Buckeyes prepared to face Wisconsin and its new head coach, Gary Andersen, in their Big Ten opener, Meyer was sarcastically asked by a reporter if he missed Bielema.

"No, I'm good with Gary," Meyer said with a laugh.

"The feeling's mutual," Bielema would respond later that week during an appearance on ESPN's *College Football Live*.

In his first four seasons in Fayetteville, Bielema has amassed just a 25–26 record, including a 10–22 mark in SEC play. He's seldom crossed paths with Meyer since, save for Ohio State hiring away his defensive coordinator, Chris Ash, following the 2013 campaign and a couple of mutual targets on the recruiting trail. As far as Bielema and Meyer's respective career trajectories are concerned, Meyer enters 2017 as one of the sport's most prominent and successful coaches, while Bielema is battling to stay off of the hot seat heading into his fifth season with the Hogs.

Bielema would briefly find himself in the crosshairs of Buckeyes fans once again at the start of the 2015 campaign, when he pointed out that Ohio State was slated to play just one ranked opponent for the rest of the season, while the Razorbacks were set to face eight. But just a week later, Bielema's argument would prove null and void, as Toledo upset then–No. 18 Arkansas.

Bielema making a vocal proclamation only to have the results on the field fail to back him up? It was par for the course as far as his rivalry with the Buckeye State was concerned.

★ ★ ★

Urban Meyer vs. Mark Dantonio

Entering the second-to-last game of the 2016 regular season, the respective records of Ohio State and Michigan State hardly would have indicated a rivalry game was about to take place.

The Buckeyes were 9–1 and appeared to be in pole position to secure a spot in the College Football Playoff. The Spartans, meanwhile, laid claim to just a 3–7 mark on the season after entering the year with high expectations following a playoff appearance of their own.

Yet with the way Urban Meyer described Michigan State in the days leading up to his team's trip to East Lansing, you would never have known the Spartans were struggling.

"All focus and laser lights are on a team that we know very well, a lot of respect for," Meyer said. "Excellent players, great coaches, and we're going to do our very best to perform well on the road."

What was more was that it didn't seem like lip service or coach-speak—you could believe what Meyer was saying.

After all, no program in the Big Ten has given Meyer's Buckeyes as many problems since he arrived in Columbus as Mark Dantonio's Michigan State teams have.

In the first five Meyer–Dantonio matchups, Ohio State has held a 3–2 advantage, but the Spartans have had plenty to show for them, including two Big Ten championships over that span. All five matchups have been extremely physical and highly competitive, with the Buckeyes barely holding a 121–120 scoring advantage over the course of the five contests.

Yet despite the evenness to which their teams have played, Meyer and Dantonio have taken different paths to building their programs into two of the Big Ten's best. For Dantonio, the hard-nosed foundation in which he's built his Michigan State program—and that has given the Buckeyes so many problems in their first five seasons under Meyer—has been a common theme throughout his coaching career.

Born in El Paso, Texas, but raised in Ohio, Dantonio earned all-state honors as a defensive back at Zanesville High School, where his father served as the school's baseball and basketball coach. South Carolina head coach Jim Carlen successfully recruited Dantonio to Columbia out of high school and he spent three seasons as a reserve safety for the Gamecocks from 1976 to '78.

"He was very hard-nosed as a player," Dantonio's position coach, Dale Evans told the *Cincinnati Enquirer* in 2004. "He was one of those guys that never said very much but was always absorbing everything you were telling him. He understood what his physical limitations were and knew that if he was going to play, he needed to have an edge on knowing his assignment and knowing what everybody else is supposed to be doing."

Dantonio was never the type of talent that would be bound for the NFL and knew before his playing career had even come to an end that he wanted to get into coaching. After his time in Columbia had come to an end, Dantonio returned to the Buckeye State, joining Brian Burke's program at Ohio University as a graduate assistant. In his lone season in Athens, the Bobcats compiled a 6–5 record before Dantonio departed for his first venture in the Big Ten, joining College Football Hall of Famer Jim Young's staff at Purdue as a graduate assistant.

The Boilermakers, however, would struggle throughout a 5–6 season, leading to Young resigning at the end of the campaign. In 1982, Dantonio got his first taste as a full-time coach as the defensive coordinator at

Butler Community College in El Dorado, Kansas, before returning to the grad-assistant ranks on Earle Bruce's Ohio State staff in 1983.

While in Columbus, Dantonio would meet a young quarterbacks coach named Jim Tressel, who would prove to be an instrumental figure in his coaching career.

After spending a season as the defensive backs coach on Jim Dennison's staff at the University of Akron, Dantonio would reunite with Tressel as the defensive coordinator at Youngstown State University, where Tressel had taken over as the head coach in 1986. After five seasons with the FCS Penguins, Dantonio returned to the FBS level in 1991, when another one of his former coworkers in Columbus, Glen Mason, hired him as the defensive backs coach at Kansas.

From 1991 to '94, the Jayhawks compiled a 25–21 record as Dantonio helped develop defensive backs Tim Hill and Gerald McBurrows into NFL draft picks. That would prove to become a common theme throughout his coaching career.

If Tressel was the most influential figure in Dantonio's rise to becoming a head coach, then the second most is Nick Saban, who hired the 39-year-old assistant as his defensive backs coach at Michigan State in 1995. Although for the most part, the Spartans were mired in mediocrity throughout his first stint in East Lansing, Dantonio received a crash course in running a program from Saban, who would prove to become one of the sport's all-time greats.

"I had the opportunity to work with a guy who had been in the NFL and had obviously a lot of success as a coordinator in the NFL," Dantonio said of his experience working for Saban. "So my knowledge in the secondary grew greatly in those five years. I appreciate everything that he's done for me in that vein."

Said Saban of his time working alongside Dantonio: "I thought we were fortunate to be able to hire him and he did a fantastic job for us in the five years that we were there."

After Saban left for the head coaching job at LSU in 2000, Dantonio remained in East Lansing, working on Bobby Williams' Michigan State staff as the Spartans struggled to a 5–6 record. The following off-season, he would catch arguably the biggest break of his coaching career, as Tressel took over for John Cooper as the head coach at Ohio State and hired his former Youngstown State colleague as the Buckeyes' new defensive coordinator.

It was back in Columbus that Dantonio became one of the hottest assistant coaches in all of college football.

After leading Ohio State's defense to a top-20 ranking in 2001, Dantonio engineered the nation's No. 2–ranked unit in 2002 as the Buckeyes compiled a 14–0 record and upset Miami (Florida) in the Fiesta Bowl to win the program's first national championship in more than 30 years.

In 2003, Ohio State's defense dropped to No. 16 nationally, but remained stockpiled with what would become premier NFL talent. From 2001 to '03, Dantonio helped develop 13 defenders into NFL draft picks, including first-round selections Will Smith and Chris Gamble. He also played a role in stockpiling the Buckeyes' roster with talent on the recruiting trail, helping lure the likes of A.J. Hawk, Bobby Carpenter, and Donte Whitner to Columbus.

After three seasons as the defensive coordinator at one of college football's premier programs and at 48 years old, Dantonio got his first crack as a head coach when the University of Cincinnati hired him to replace Rick Minter.

In 2004, the Bearcats compiled a 7–5 record, including a win over Marshall in the Fort Worth Bowl, as Dantonio became the first

Cincinnati coach in 23 years to record a winning record in his debut season. The following year, the Bearcats would go just 4–7 in their debut season in the Big East, before bouncing back to 7–5 in 2006.

During his time in the Queen City, Dantonio furthered his trend of developing NFL talent, putting players like Trent Cole, Brent Celek, and Daven Holly in the pros. And on the recruiting trail, he laid the foundation for a program that would go on to reach double-digit wins in five of the next six seasons.

Dantonio, however, wouldn't be around to see the success he set the table for in Cincinnati through. At the end of the 2006 season, Michigan State hired him as its new head coach following the firing of John L. Smith.

It wouldn't take long to find out that Dantonio would be a perfect fit running the show for the Spartans. In 2008, Michigan State won nine games, marking both the Spartans' most wins and the first time they finished a season ranked since Saban's final year in East Lansing in 1999.

After a disappointing 6–7 record in 2009, Michigan State won the inaugural Big Ten title game—the Spartans' first conference championship in 20 years. Michigan State would repeat as division champions the following year before falling to Wisconsin in Indianapolis, but finished the season ranked No. 10 after a win over Georgia in the Outback Bowl.

In 2012, six Spartans—including quarterback Kirk Cousins—were selected in the NFL draft, which marked the most players from Michigan State in a single draft since 2000. All the while, Dantonio turned the tables on his program's contentious rivalry with Michigan, as Michigan State earned four straight wins over the Wolverines from 2008 to 2011 and seven of eight matchups against Michigan from 2008 to 2015.

By the time the 2012 season had arrived, Dantonio had developed the Spartans into what was undisputedly considered one of the top programs in the Big Ten. But it wasn't until 2013—and his second matchup with Meyer—that the Michigan State head coach could say his program had arrived on a national level.

That all changed on December 7, 2013, as the No. 10 Spartans squared off with No. 2 Ohio State, which was riding a 24-game winning streak and just one win away from clinching a BCS Championship Game appearance in its second season under Meyer.

But while the Buckeyes entered the game as a six-point favorite, Michigan State's physicality seemed to stifle Ohio State as the Spartans jumped out to a 17–0 lead. The Buckeyes would bounce back to score 24 unanswered points and held a 24–20 lead entering the fourth quarter.

It was then that the resiliency of the MSU program under Dantonio was most apparent, as the Spartans scored 10 unanswered fourth-quarter points, punching their ticket to Pasadena and the Rose Bowl in the process.

After beating Stanford 24–20 in the "Grandaddy of Them All," Michigan State would finish the season ranked No. 3 in the nation—the Spartans' highest year-end ranking since 1966.

"Our plan is to keep winning. Our plan is that we're one game away," Dantonio said after the game. "I said, 'Why not us?' a couple weeks ago. I think we can compete with anybody in this country."

With key starters like quarterback Connor Cook and defensive end Shilique Calhoun back the following season, Michigan State would remain in the national title picture until early November, when Meyer's Buckeyes exacted their revenge, beating the Spartans 49–37 en route to winning the inaugural College Football Playoff championship. The following year, however, Michigan State—this time behind the play of backup quarterback Tyler O'Connor—would once again play the role of spoiler, beating top-ranked and defending national champion Ohio State in Columbus to bring the Buckeyes' playoff hopes to an end in 2015.

Two weeks later, the Spartans topped Iowa in Indianapolis 16–13 to clinch their third Big Ten championship under Dantonio and a spot in the College Football Playoff. Ultimately, however, No. 3 Michigan State wouldn't seem to possess enough firepower to keep up with Saban's No. 2 Alabama, as the eventual national champions beat the Spartans 38–0.

After compiling a 55–16 record from 2010 to 2015, Michigan State would hit a skid in 2016, losing seven consecutive games after a 2–0 start to the season. Yet despite being seemingly outmanned following the departures of Cook, Calhoun, and first-round left tackle Jack Conklin, there the Spartans were, once again primed to throw a wrench in the Buckeyes' championship plans.

On a windy, late-November day in East Lansing, Ohio State running back Mike Weber broke a 10-all tie with a 4-yard touchdown run in the third quarter, but the Buckeyes soon found themselves on the ropes. After Michigan State running back L.J. Scott scored a one-yard run with 4:53 remaining in the game, Dantonio kept his offense on the field to attempt a two-point conversion to try to take the lead.

But on the ensuing play, Ohio State linebacker Chris Worley picked off O'Connor and an interception by Buckeyes cornerback Gareon Conley later in the fourth quarter would go on to seal the game. Yet despite the Spartans' unimpressive record, no one in the Ohio State locker room after the game seemed surprised that it took another close call against a Dantonio-coached team to keep the Buckeyes' playoff hopes alive.

"I watch film like everybody else and their record didn't show the team we saw today. People look at records and think we should blow them out but that's not the case," said Ohio State quarterback J.T. Barrett. "They get up for us."

It's been a common theme through Dantonio's tenure in East Lansing and Meyer's time in Columbus, despite the Spartans hardly recruiting at the same clip as the Buckeyes—or Michigan, for that matter. Instead,

Michigan State has relied on its tried and tested player development program, which has helped turn former 3-star recruiting prospects like Darqueze Dennard and Trae Waynes.

Dantonio's approach has led to a modern golden age of sorts for the Spartans, who have amassed a 90–42 in the first 10 years under the direction of their head coach.

"He's certainly done a better job than I ever did there, I'll tell you that," Saban said in advance of their playoff meeting.

As far as how his career compares with Meyer's, Dantonio trails the Buckeyes head coach in most notable statistical categories. In 13 seasons as a head coach, the now-60-year-old Dantonio has compiled a 108–59 record, good for a .647 winning percentage, including a 5–5 mark in bowl games while coaching four consensus All-Americans and putting 31 players in the pros as draft picks.

But when it comes to head-to-head contests, no coach in his current conference has been as evenly matched with Meyer as Dantonio has been. What Saban was to Meyer in the SEC, Dantonio has since become in the Big Ten, creating a rivalry that's played out every bit as much on the sidelines as it has on the field.

Urban Meyer vs. Jim Harbaugh

At his introductory press conference at Ohio State, Urban Meyer mentioned the coach who would go on to become his chief coaching rival in his time as the Buckeyes' head coach.

He just didn't know it at the time.

Asked for his take on Ohio State's storied rival with Michigan, Meyer reminisced back to the 1986 edition of "The Game," his first as an Ohio State graduate assistant. With a trip to Pasadena to play in the Rose Bowl on the line, the Buckeyes would lose to the Wolverines 26–24—but the game is just as much remembered for the guarantee made by the Michigan starting quarterback as it is for its outcome.

"I understand the significance of it," Meyer said of the rivalry. "And I remember my experience in that game was the first year when Jim Harbaugh guaranteed to win here in Ohio Stadium."

At the time, nothing seemed noteworthy about Meyer mentioning Harbaugh. After all, the former Wolverines signal-caller was just wrapping up his final season at Stanford at the time before taking over as the head coach of the San Francisco 49ers.

But four years after Ohio State introduced Meyer as its new head coach and 28 years after Harbaugh's infamous guarantee, the two would cross paths once again when Harbaugh took over as the head coach at his alma mater, beginning a new chapter in college football's most storied rivalry.

Thus far, the two coaches have only met twice in head-to-head match-ups, with each contest providing a memorable outcome. Their rivalry has also extended to the recruiting trail, where Meyer and Harbaugh have battled over the top prospects in the Midwest, while bringing a national flair to Big Ten recruiting.

Even over the course of Harbaugh's short tenure in Ann Arbor, no two coaches in the conference have done more to bring national attention to the Big Ten than Meyer and Harbaugh have.

Dating back to his college career, Harbaugh has always had a habit of generating headlines. And while Meyer worked his way up the coaching ranks before taking a more prominent presence in the

114

Ohio State–Michigan rivalry, Harbaugh followed a more unusual path through the football world before regaining his.

The son of former Michigan assistant coach Jack Harbaugh, Jim Harbaugh was born in Toledo's old Mercy Hospital on December 23, 1963—seven months after Meyer was delivered by the exact same doctor in the exact same hospital. Weird, huh?

Alongside his older brother, John, Jim would spend the early part of his life in northwest Ohio, where Jack served as the head coach at Eaton High School and Xenia High School, before a brief stint as an assistant at Moorehead State.

In 1968, the Harbaugh family returned to the Toledo area when Jack joined Don Nehlen's staff at Bowling Green as an assistant. Jack would spend three seasons with the Falcons before joining Ray Nagel's staff at Iowa.

It was the seven seasons Jack spent as Michigan's defensive backs coach under legendary head coach Bo Schembechler, however, that Jim remembers most. Growing up in Ann Arbor, Jim was an avid athlete and, of course, a Wolverines fan, and he was actually once caught running on to the field to celebrate a touchdown scored by Michigan star quarterback Ron Leach.

"We had the run of the golf course," Harbaugh said of his childhood in Ann Arbor. "There was a basement that had putting greens, sandboxes, and baseball batting cages, and for three weeks it was heaven on earth."

In 1980, Jack accepted a job to become the defensive coordinator on Paul Wiggins' first staff at Stanford. As a result, Jim spent the second half of his promising prep career playing at Palo Alto High School, before returning to Ann Arbor to play for Schembechler at Michigan in 1982.

Harbaugh's playing career with the Wolverines, however, got off to a rocky start, as he was 10 minutes late to his first team meeting.

"Coach Schembechler told me I would never play a single down at the University of Michigan my entire career," Harbaugh recalled.

For at least one season, that remained true, as Harbaugh would red-shirt the 1982 campaign with Steve Smith and Dave Hall ahead of him on the depth chart. He enjoyed only limited playing time the following year as well, attempting just five passes on the season as he remained No. 3 on the Wolverines' depth chart.

After beating out Chris Zurbrugg and Russ Rein in spring practice, Harbaugh entered the 1984 season as the Wolverines' starting signal-caller. In his first start, the sophomore helped lead Michigan to a 22–14 win over top-ranked defending national champion Miami (Florida) and star quarterback Bernie Kosar.

The Wolverines would fall to Washington the following week, before beating Big Ten foes Indiana and Wisconsin. Throwing for 718 yards, three touchdowns, and five interceptions, Harbaugh's stint as Michigan's starting quarterback had gotten off to a promising start, but a broken arm suffered against Michigan State would bring his sophomore season to an unceremonious end.

Harbaugh returned to the Wolverines' starting lineup the following season, leading Michigan to a 10–1–1 record, including a 27–23 win over Nebraska in the Fiesta Bowl to close the campaign. In his first full season of action, Harbaugh emerged as one of the nation's top passers, compiling a nation-high passing efficiency rating of 163.7.

In his final three games of his junior year, Harbaugh looked particularly impressive, completing 41-of-50 passes for 706 yards, nine touchdowns, and no interceptions in wins over Minnesota, Ohio State, and Nebraska. It would prove to be just a sign of things to come the following year.

As a senior, Harbaugh became a legitimate Heisman Trophy contender, as the Wolverines opened the season on a nine-game winning streak. A loss to Minnesota in the 10th week of the season, however, would knock Michigan out of the national title hunt, a week prior to heading to Columbus for a bout with the No. 7 Buckeyes.

Speaking to reporters in the days leading up to the game, it was then that Harbaugh's inherent confidence first made national headlines.

"We're going to play in the Rose Bowl this year, I guarantee it. We'll beat Ohio State and we'll be in Pasadena on January 1," Harbaugh said.

Completing 19 of his 29 passes for 261 yards, Harbaugh made good on his promise, as the Wolverines won the game on a missed Matt Frantz

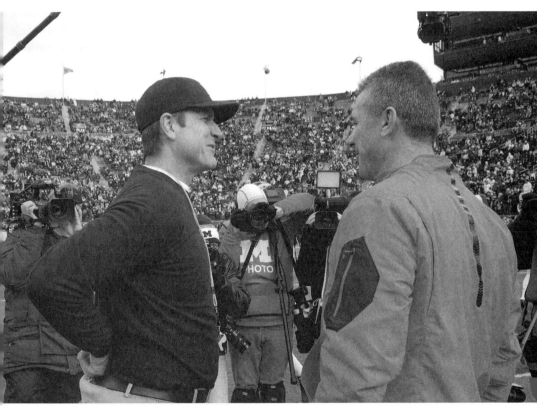

Meyer and Jim Harbaugh have renewed national interest in one of college football's top rivalries, the University of Michigan and Ohio State.

field-goal attempt. With that, he forever etched himself in Ohio State–Michigan lore.

"I actually remember it very well," Meyer said in 2016. "[Former OSU running back] Vince Workman had a touchdown, and we missed a field goal right at the end."

Harbaugh would go on to finish No. 3 in Heisman Trophy voting behind Miami (Florida) quarterback Vinny Testaverde and Temple's Paul Palmer, while winning the *Chicago Tribune*'s Silver Football trophy, which is awarded each season to the Big Ten MVP. The Wolverines would finish the season ranked No. 8 in the country with an 11–2 record following a loss to Arizona State in the Rose Bowl.

In 1987, the Chicago Bears selected Harbaugh with the No. 26 overall pick of the NFL draft. He'd spend seven seasons in the Windy City, where he considered legendary head coach Mike Ditka to be one of the early influencers in his coaching career.

"So many things," Harbaugh answered at Big Ten media days in 2015 when asked what he's learned from Ditka. "It's your coach. It's your coach. When you're a player, your coach is—it's like family."

Harbaugh's NFL playing days would ultimately last the span of 14 seasons, including time with the Indianapolis Colts, Baltimore Ravens, and San Diego Chargers. The highlight of his pro playing days would come in 1995, when he earned first-team All-Pro honors and won the AP Comeback Player of the Year award while leading the Colts to a 9–7 record and appearance in the AFC Championship Game.

Harbaugh didn't even wait for his playing days to come to an end before jump-starting his coaching career. From 1994 to 2001, Harbaugh served as an NCAA-certified, unpaid assistant at Western Kentucky, where his father served as the team's head coach from 1989 to 2002. Jim's duties included scouting and recruiting players, including 17 prospects who were ultimately a part of the Hilltoppers' 2002 Division I-AA national title team.

In his first full season of retirement as a player, Harbaugh joined Bill Callahan's staff with the Oakland Raiders as a quarterbacks coach, helping Rich Gannon earn MVP honors in 2002. After Harbaugh's debut season on the sidelines ended in a Super Bowl loss to the Tampa Bay Buccaneers, his ascent up the coaching ranks would prove to be a quick one. Harbaugh spent just one more season in Oakland before the University of San Diego hired him as its head coach in 2004.

Harbaugh's first head coaching job was hardly a glamorous one. The FCS-level Toreros had enjoyed an 8–2 season in 2003, which was followed by the departure of longtime head coach Kevin McGarry, who would later claim that the school had forced him to retire.

In his first season at San Diego, Harbaugh's Toreros would start the season on a 2–4 skid, but won their final five games to amass a 7–4 record. Harbaugh's success in San Diego would continue into 2005, as the Toreros reached unprecedented heights as a program, recording an 11–1 record and winning their first Pioneer Football League conference championship in school history.

San Diego would repeat as PFL champions in 2006 as Harbaugh developed quarterback Josh Johnson into an All-American and eventual fifth-round pick in the NFL draft.

With a 22–2 record over the course of two seasons, Harbaugh was a rising star in the coaching ranks. In 2007, he'd make the leap to the Division I FBS level when Stanford hired him to replace Walt Harris, who had gone just 6–17 in his two seasons in charge of the Cardinal.

The ramifications of five consecutive losing seasons on the Stanford roster were apparent. Harbaugh's first Cardinal team went 4–8 in 2007, but also earned his first signature win as a head coach when they beat top-ranked USC 24–23 as a 41-point underdog. At Pac-10 media days earlier that year, Harbaugh had referred to the Trojans as "the best team in the country and maybe the best team in the history of college football."

Stanford would slightly improve to 5–7 in 2008, but in 2009, Harbaugh had the Cardinal's recruiting and player development rolling. His first prized quarterback prospect, Andrew Luck, was developing into one of the nation's top signal-callers and running back Toby Gerhart would go on to become the runner-up for the Heisman Trophy, finishing behind only Alabama running back Mark Ingram in voting.

After not having a player picked in either the 2008 or 2009 drafts, a combined 11 players from Stanford would be selected from 2010 to '12, including Luck, the top overall pick of the 2012 draft.

The Cardinal recorded an 8–5 record in 2009—its first winning season since 2001—including a 55–21 win at No. 11 USC, marking head coach Pete Carroll's first November loss with the Trojans. During the game Harbaugh attempted to run up the score by attempting a two-point conversion with the outcome of the contest already apparent. Afterward, the two would share a not-so-friendly handshake.

"I just honestly thought there was an opportunity coming off the ball, the way our backs were running and the way we were playing," Harbaugh would attempt to explain, per the Associated Press.

It marked the first time in his coaching career Harbaugh's fiery personality would make an appearance on the national level.

In 2010, Stanford put together arguably its greatest season in program history, tallying a 12–1 record, including a decisive 40–12 win over Virginia Tech in the Orange Bowl to close the campaign.

As Meyer returned to the college ranks following his one-season sabbatical, Harbaugh would make his return to the NFL, as he took over as the head coach of the San Francisco 49ers.

It was there that Harbaugh's intensity became most apparent as he became one of the most famous coaches in all of football. From 2011 to

'13, Harbaugh led the 49ers to three consecutive NFC Championship Games, including an appearance in Super Bowl XLVII, where San Francisco lost to the Baltimore Ravens, who were coached by Jim's brother, John.

Despite amassing an impressive 44–19–1 record and two division titles in four seasons with the 49ers, Harbaugh was let go after the 2014 season following a power struggle with general manager Trent Baalke. It wouldn't take long for him to find a landing spot, however, as two days after coaching his final game for San Francisco, Harbaugh was introduced—or reintroduced—at Michigan as the Wolverines' new head coach.

"There are very special words that are in the English language that we all embrace. There's family. There's friends. There's teammates. There's victory," Harbaugh said. "I was reminded of another very special word when I was driving into Ann Arbor this morning, and that word is homecoming. Our family's had three homecomings to Ann Arbor, Michigan, in my lifetime."

As Meyer was in the process of winning the inaugural College Football Playoff and his third national championship, Harbaugh hit the recruiting trail and started a Twitter account to display his unique personality.

In the lead up to his first National Signing Day in Ann Arbor, one of Harbaugh's primary targets was a Detroit running back named Mike Weber, who had flipped his commitment from Michigan to Ohio State following the firing of Wolverines head coach Brady Hoke. Harbaugh's efforts, however, would prove to be too little, too late, as Weber ultimately signed with the rival Buckeyes.

This would lead to the first run-in between Harbaugh and his new rival, Meyer, after Ohio State running backs coach Stan Drayton departed for the NFL the day after Weber had sent in his National Letter of Intent.

With Weber's pledge to the Buckeyes in doubt as rumors swirled that he would attempt to get out of his now-binding commitment, Harbaugh sent out a tweet that many perceived to be aimed at Meyer.

"Thought of the day—What a tangled web we weave when first we practice to deceive!—Sir Walter Scott," Harbaugh posted.

Members of the Ohio State staff would respond with their own not-so-subtle social media posts, including pictures of the Buckeyes' newly won national title trophy. Ultimately, Weber's dramatic recruitment would come to a quiet end as Ohio State smoothed things over with the four-star running back.

Plus, it didn't hurt that Harbaugh was often making noise of his own. Before ever coaching in a game, Harbaugh made waves both with his Twitter account, where he interacted with celebrities like Judge Judy and pro wrestling legend Ric Flair, and on the recruiting trail, where he initiated an inventive nine-stop, seven-state tour of satellite camps, which were attended by some of the nation's top prospects.

The practice drew criticism from the SEC, which at the time outlawed the practice of satellite camps. And while Meyer didn't necessarily agree with Harbaugh's camps, the Ohio State head coach also wasn't going to be left behind, as the Buckeyes went on to hold one of their own in Boca Raton, Florida, in 2015.

"If it helps us, we'll do it," he said.

On the field, Harbaugh's first Michigan team would lose its season opener to Utah before winning five straight games heading into a rivalry contest against Michigan State. But while the No. 12 Wolverines appeared to have the No. 7 Spartans beat, a botched punt on the final play of the game would lead to the unlikeliest of Michigan State victories.

Still in contention for a Big Ten title—and perhaps even a playoff spot—Michigan would go on to win four straight games heading into Harbaugh's first head-to-head matchup with Meyer. With a share of the

Big Ten East title on the line for both teams, it figured to be the first of many high-stakes matchups between the Big Ten's two most prominent head coaches.

Harbaugh's first appearance in The Game as a head coach, however, was hardly an instant classic, as the Buckeyes handed the Wolverines a lopsided 42–13 loss inside of Michigan Stadium. From there, Michigan would go on to beat Florida in the Citrus Bowl to finish the season at 10–3—twice as many wins as the Wolverines recorded a season before.

In 2016, Harbaugh's yearlong stint in the spotlight paid off as he signed the nation's No. 5–ranked recruiting class, which included the nation's top prospect, five-star defensive lineman Rashan Gary. After hosting a celebrity-packed "Signing with the Stars" event to commemorate the class, complete with cameos from Flair, Tom Brady, and Derek Jeter, Harbaugh then kicked up his attention-grabbing efforts thanks to public Twitter-fueled feuds with Alabama's Nick Saban, Georgia head coach Kirby Smart, and even Ohio State athletic director Gene Smith. The primary conflict between Harbaugh and his colleagues? His relentless approach on the recruiting trail, as he controversially took his team down to Florida for a week of spring practice and quadrupled his satellite-camp schedule for the summer.

"Somebody made a joke about us and our program," Harbaugh said of a tweet aimed at Smith, who had insinuated that Michigan's spring practice plans were a result of the Wolverines still rebuilding. "And we fired one back over their bow. I think that's warranted."

On the field, Harbaugh gave onlookers something to talk about as well, as Michigan entered the season ranked No. 7 and would rise to as high as No. 2 on the heels of nine straight wins to start the campaign. The Wolverines, however, would lose two of their final three regular season contests, including a second matchup with Meyer—a double-overtime edition of The Game that punched the Buckeyes' ticket to the College

Football Playoff and prevented the Wolverines from clinching a spot in the Big Ten title game.

Afterward, Harbaugh harped on the officials, who he felt had missed several key calls in the game. Meyer, meanwhile, referred to their second meeting as one of the rivalry's all-time classics.

"That is one of the classic games of this rivalry that will forever be, because I know this rivalry as well as anybody," Meyer said. "That game is right in there. I'm not saying it's the greatest, because that's disrespectful for the other players that have played in it. But that's an instant classic between two great teams. We knew going in it was going to be that way."

The Wolverines would close the season with a 33–32 loss to Florida State in the Orange Bowl, bringing Michigan's three losses on the year to total margin of five points. But by the end of the 2016 campaign, it had already become clear that the Wolverines were once again one of college football's top programs.

On National Signing Day, Harbaugh signed a second straight top-five class, beating out Meyer for five-star receiver Donovan Peoples-Jones, who hails from the same high school Weber did two years prior. The Buckeyes, however, would ultimately sign the higher-ranked class for the third straight year since Harbaugh arrived in Ann Arbor.

When it comes to their respective résumés, Meyer and Harbaugh's career numbers are tough to compare, due largely to Meyer's head start and Harbaugh's four-year stint in the NFL. In any comparison, however, Meyer maintains an edge when it comes to his head-to-head victories over Harbaugh both on the field and the recruiting trail. While Harbaugh has reinvigorated his alma mater in two short seasons, he still has yet to reach the heights of Meyer, who has built a juggernaut in Columbus.

Yet he remains the biggest threat to Meyer in the Big Ten, as Harbaugh's name nevertheless belongs in the conversation of college football's top active head coaches, alongside the likes of Meyer, Saban, and Dabo Swinney. Thanks to his aggressive approach, resourceful recruiting, player-development prowess, and history of winning, so long as Harbaugh is in Ann Arbor, the Wolverines will remain a force to be reckoned with in the years to come.

Just like Michigan's victory over the Buckeyes in 1986, it's guaranteed.

PART III

★ ★ ★

Urban Meyer
vs. His Idols

Urban Meyer is inherently new school.

He favors recruiting over tradition. He runs a spread offense that rarely requires his quarterback to line up behind center. He doesn't have a signature sweater vest or ball cap—he just wears whatever Nike gives him.

But while Urban Meyer might as well be the face of the modern college football coach, his rise through the coaching ranks can also be traced to some of the sport's most storied figures. Be it his childhood in Ashtabula, where he idolized Woody Hayes and Bo Schembechler during the "Ten Year War;" his time at Notre Dame, where he learned under Lou Holtz; or even his final game at Florida, where he coached against one of his longtime idols, Meyer's life and career have possessed no shortage of links to some of college football's biggest legends.

Given all he has accomplished, Meyer's career undoubtedly stacks up against—and even surpasses—some of the very coaches he grew up idolizing.

As much as Meyer has thrived in rivalries, he's never been shy to pay homage.

Urban Meyer vs. Jim Tressel

In what was considered to be the high point of Urban Meyer's debut season in Columbus, the loudest ovation inside of Ohio Stadium came not for the Buckeyes' current head coach or the actual team out on the field, but the coach whom Meyer had replaced.

It was November 24, 2012, and Ohio State was in the midst of Meyer's first game against the "Team Up North." On the line for the Buckeyes was an undefeated season—and not much else. Ohio State had been barred from postseason play due to NCAA violations committed by former players and its former head coach.

Ohio State would win the game 26–21 behind 146 rushing yards from running back Carlos Hyde. And in an odd twist of irony, the former head coach at least partly responsible for the Buckeyes' 2012 campaign's stopping at 12 games wasn't just in attendance for an Ohio State game for the first time in nearly two years—he was also honored.

While Buckeyes fans cheered for Hyde's bulldozing runs and Braxton Miller's spectacular, highlight-reel athleticism, nothing compared to the ovation Jim Tressel received as he trotted out onto the field between the first and second quarters of the 2012 edition of The Game. What was originally intended to be a moment honoring the 10th anniversary of Ohio State's last national title team quickly transformed into a Tressel love fest, as his ex-players hoisted their former head coach onto their shoulders much to the adulation of 105,899 in attendance.

It some ways, the day simultaneously marked the unofficial end of one era in Columbus and an exclamation on the birth of another. Given their head-to-head meeting in a national title game six years prior and that Meyer would go on to become Tressel's full-time successor at Ohio State, the respective legacies of the two beloved Buckeyes head coaches will always be linked.

Yet despite each growing up Ohio State fans and having even shared mentors throughout their own rises through the coaching ranks, Meyer and Tressel have achieved their success in Columbus via vastly different approaches. And as the cheers inside of Ohio Stadium on that November afternoon showed, no matter how much Meyer wins, he may never connect with Buckeyes fans the same way that his predecessor did.

Jim Tressel was born into coaching—specifically, Ohio college football coaching. His father, Lee Tressel, was one of the most successful coaches in Ohio high school history, thanks to stints at Mentor High School and Ohio prep powerhouse Massillon Washington. In 1958, the elder Tressel took over as the head coach at Division III Baldwin Wallace, where he would go on to win a national title in 1978.

Due to his father's hectic work schedule, Jim wasn't able to spend much time with Lee growing up—except for when Ohio State played Michigan at the end of each season, as the Yellow Jackets' season had usually already ended.

"It was the one time of the season we knew we'd get to see him," Jim told the *New York Times* in 2007.

A star quarterback at Berea High School, Jim would go on to play for his father at Baldwin Wallace from 1971 to '74, earning All–Ohio Conference honors in his senior season.

After his playing days had come to an end, it didn't take long for Jim to join his father in the coaching ranks as a graduate assistant on Jim Dennison's staff at the University of Akron. Tressel would spend three seasons in the Rubber City before being hired by Miami (Ohio) head coach Tom Reed as a quarterbacks and wide receivers coach in 1979.

Head coach Dick MacPherson hired Tressel as his first quarterbacks coach at Syracuse in 1981, but Tressel's stint in New York would be a short stay. After the Orangemen struggled to a 2–9 record in 1982, Tressel returned to his home state, joining Earle Bruce's Ohio State staff as the Buckeyes' quarterbacks and wide receivers coach in 1983.

"He's got a great football background," Bruce told TheOzone.net of Tressel in 2001. "His dad was a great friend and a great coach. When you mention the name Tressel, that pops out at you when you are coaching.

"He's straight with everybody, and he knows how to deal with people. He's a no-B.S. guy. He's focused and gets the job done."

It was in Columbus that Tressel tasted his first real success as a coach at the college level. From 1983 to '85, the Buckeyes compiled a combined 27–9 record, going 9–3 for three consecutive seasons and winning a Big Ten championship in 1984. In that span, Tressel played a large part in the development of quarterback Mike Tomczak, as well as future Ohio State starter Jim Karsatos. Beginning in 1984, he also began coaching the Buckeyes' running backs, helping Keith Byars finish No. 2 in Heisman Trophy voting that very same year.

Tressel ultimately spent three seasons working under Bruce, just missing the start of Meyer's tenure as a graduate assistant by a year. In 1986, Youngstown State University hired Tressel to replace Bill Narduzzi as its head coach.

Tressel's tenure with the Division I-AA Penguins would get off to a rocky start as they struggled to a 2–9 record in his debut campaign. In 1987, YSU improved to 8–4 and made the Division I-AA playoffs for the first time since 1979, a feat the Penguins would accomplish in seven of Tressel's first nine seasons on the sidelines.

After failing to advance past the quarterfinals in any of its first three appearances, Youngstown State would win its first national championship in program history in 1991 following a win over Marshall in the national title game. The Penguins would once again reach the title game the following year, but their bid to repeat fell short thanks to a 31–28 defeat at the hands of the Thundering Herd. In 1993, Youngstown State and Marshall would square off with the national title for the third straight year, with the Penguins exacting revenge with a 17–5 victory for their second national championship in three seasons.

Tressel's reign was just beginning.

From 1987 to 2000, Tressel amassed four national titles, five conference titles, 10 playoff appearances, and an overall record of 135–57–2. He was named the Division I-AA Coach of the Year in 1991, 1993, 1994, and 1997, and his Youngstown State's four national titles were at the time the second most in Division I-AA (now known as FCS) history, trailing only Georgia Southern (North Dakota State has since won five).

By any measure, Tressel had become one of the most successful coaches in all of football, at any level. But his time with the Penguins wasn't without controversy.

In 1998, Tressel's former star quarterback, Ray Isaac, admitted to accepting significant benefits from a former chairman of the Youngstown State board of trustees. The Penguins were ultimately docked scholarships

Meyer's Florida Gators defeated Jim Tressel's Ohio State Buckeyes 41–14 in the 2007 BCS National Championship Game. In 2011, Meyer would become Tressel's successor at the helm of the Buckeyes.

for the infraction, but allowed to keep their 1991 national title as the statute of limitations had run out. The NCAA also faulted Tressel and YSU for their initial investigation into the allegations in 1994, but fell short of citing each for wrongdoing.

It wouldn't be the last controversy of Tressel's career.

In 2001, he'd make the leap to major-college football when Ohio State hired him to replace John Cooper as its head coach following the 2000 season. At the time, Tressel was an unknown to most college football fans, including many in Columbus.

Throughout their search for Tressel's successor, the Buckeyes had been linked to Oregon's Mike Bellotti, Stanford's Tyrone Willingam, Oakland Raiders head coach John Gruden, Minnesota's Glen Mason, and even former Ohio State linebacker Chris Spielman. But while Tressel's hiring may have seemed underwhelming to some, it didn't take long for him to win over supporters of the scarlet and gray.

At halftime of an Ohio State basketball game against Michigan following his hiring, Tressel addressed Buckeyes fans regarding his own expectations for his program.

"I can assure you that you will be proud of your young people in the classroom, in the community, and most especially in 310 days in Ann Arbor, Michigan, on the football field," he said to a raucous ovation.

Tressel proved to be a man of his word, as the Buckeyes beat the Wolverines 26–20 at the end of the season, which would mark the high point of an otherwise mundane 7–5 campaign in 2001. Tressel's emphasis on Ohio State's rival was a clear departure from his predecessor in Cooper, who had amassed a 2–10–1 record against Michigan over the course of his career in Columbus.

In 2002, the Buckeyes entered the season ranked No. 13 in the nation, thanks in large part to an experienced defense and the arrival of an impressive recruiting class, headlined by five-star running back

Maurice Clarett. Ohio State would go on to survive a series of close calls, including six games decided by seven or fewer points, and clinch an appearance in the BCS national title game Fiesta Bowl with a 14–9 win over Michigan in the final week of the regular season.

Yet despite their undefeated record, the Buckeyes entered the Fiesta Bowl as nearly a two-touchdown underdog against defending national champion Miami (Florida). The Hurricanes were stockpiled with NFL talent on both sides of the ball, including Heisman Trophy finalists in quarterback Ken Dorsey and running back Willis McGahee.

But in one of the greatest college football games ever played, Ohio State would prove to possess plenty of NFL talent of its own. Fitting in line with the Buckeyes' nail-biter of a season, the game came down to the wire with Ohio State prevailing by a score of 31–24 in double overtime.

The national championship marked the fifth of Tressel's career and Ohio State's first since 1968.

"We've always had the Best Damn Band in the Land," Tressel loudly proclaimed after the game. "Now, we have the Best Damn Team in the Land."

In just two seasons, Tressel had reasserted Ohio State's superiority over its rival, reestablished its dominance on the recruiting trail and won the Buckeyes' first since Woody Hayes was forced to step down. Eligibility issues, however, would bring Clarett's college career to a premature end and play a large part in Ohio State failing to successfully defend its national title in 2003.

After an 8–4 campaign in 2004 and 10–2 record in 2005, the Buckeyes and Heisman Trophy front-runner Troy Smith entered the 2006 season as the nation's No. 1. And for the first 12 games, Ohio State lived up to the hype, with Smith winning the Heisman Trophy as the Buckeyes punched their ticket to the BCS National Championship

Game thanks to an epic No. 1 vs. No. 2 showdown against Michigan to bring Tressel's record against the Wolverines to an impressive 5–1.

Heading back to Arizona, Ohio State found itself in a situation similar to the title game it played in five years prior—only this time, it was the Buckeyes who entered the game as heavy favorite over No. 2 Florida. And after Ted Ginn Jr. ran back the game's opening kickoff to give Ohio State a 7–0 lead, the crowning of Tressel's second national title with the Buckeyes seemed like a mere formality.

The head coach on the opposing sideline remembers it well.

"My head came off my shoulders because I saw them holding [Gators safety] Reggie Nelson right in front of me and they didn't call it," Meyer recalled. "And then I was going berserk like I have a tendency to do every once in a while, and then Brandon Siler grabs my arm—my captain—and squeezes it real hard and he says, "Coach, we're going to be all right. I got 'em. We'll be all right.'"

Florida was more than all right. The Gators would go on to beat the Buckeyes 41–14 in one of the most lopsided losses of Tressel's coaching career.

After the game, it appeared clear that while Tressel had been recruiting at a high level by Big Ten standards, he had some catching up to do when it came to acquiring talent on the national level.

"The speed on defense was instrumental," Meyer remembers. "We crushed them on the edge."

That would prove to be a common thread throughout the remainder of Tressel's tenure at Ohio State.

In 2007, the Buckeyes would get back to the national title game, but lost to another opponent from the SEC in LSU. The following two years, Ohio State would lose early out-of-conference matchups against USC, before falling short of making the national title game with an 11–1 regular season record in 2010.

As the Buckeyes prepared to take on Arkansas in the Sugar Bowl at the end of the 2010 campaign, the controversy that would ultimately lead to Tressel's ouster in Columbus was first made public.

Commonly referred to as "Tatgate," it was revealed that members of the Buckeyes roster, including star quarterback Terrelle Pryor, had sold their own Ohio State memorabilia in exchange for cash and tattoos. Later, it was found that Tressel had become aware of the infractions, but had failed to properly alert the NCAA.

Tressel had initially been hit with a two-game suspension for the 2011 season but had asked to have it extended to five to match the punishment for his players. With pressure mounting and the controversy only gaining additional exposure, Tressel resigned as Ohio State's head coach on Memorial Day 2011.

In addition to vacating the 2010 season, the NCAA slapped the Buckeyes with a one-season postseason ban and the reduction of nine total scholarships over the course of three seasons—all of which would take effect in Meyer's first year as Ohio State's head coach.

Tressel, meanwhile, was hit with a five-year show cause penalty, meaning that any school that chose to hire Tressel in the ensuing five years would have to make a case to the NCAA in order to do so and if granted, would result in Tressel sitting out his first five games, as well as any postseason games in his debut campaign.

Tressel's show cause, however, would expire without incident on December 19, 2016. After serving as a replay analyst for the Indianapolis Colts for a portion of the 2011 season, Tressel would return to Youngstown State, where he has served as the university's president since 2014.

In 2015, Tressel was inducted into the College Football Hall of Fame. Perhaps fittingly, he was first announced as an inductee at the 2015 College Football Playoff Championship Game, which also marked Meyer's first national championship victory at Ohio State.

While the Buckeyes' two most-recent full-time head coaches will always be linked, their philosophies could be perceived as vastly different.

Whereas Tressel earned the nickname the "Senator" for his habit of filibustering questions without actually saying anything of substance, Meyer has always favored a much more direct approach when it's come to dealing with the media. And while Tressel was hardly a slouch on the recruiting trail and routinely secured Ohio's top prospects and some of the best players in the Midwest, Meyer has aggressively extended the Buckeyes' efforts on a national level, which has resulted in Ohio State's landing higher-ranked classes on a more consistent basis.

When it comes to their individual coaching legacies, Meyer has reached higher heights than Tressel, winning three national championships at the Division I level. It's also certainly worth noting that Meyer has never run into trouble with the NCAA, while four of Tressel's most prominent players—Isaac, Clarett, Troy Smith, and Pryor—each had his eligibility either temporarily suspended or cut short altogether.

And of course, there's always the one head-to-head matchup between the two coaches, which Meyer's team won in lopsided fashion.

Yet when it comes to just their Ohio State legacies, one could argue that Meyer's still playing catch-up to Tressel.

While both have won national titles for the Buckeyes, Meyer's one Big Ten title trails Tressel's seven—counting the one vacated in 2010— although Tressel's time in Columbus predated the creation of the Big Ten Championship Game. With a tenure twice as long, Tressel recorded a record of 106–22, while through five seasons at Ohio State, Meyer's record with the Buckeyes stands at 61–6.

How Meyer ultimately measures up to Tressel in Ohio State lore will largely depend on how long he remains in Columbus. His .910 winning percentage with the Buckeyes tops Tressel's mark of .828 and, for those keeping score, his 5–0 against "That Team Up North" still trails Tressel's 9–1 record against Ohio State's chief rival.

But regardless of how their career statistics—both in Columbus and outside—measure up against one another, there's no denying that each holds a unique place in the hearts of Buckeye fans.

For Meyer, the creation of his Ohio State legacy is still well under way. As for Tressel, despite his perceived wrongdoing and resulting sanctions, he'll always remain a fan favorite in Columbus due to his unique connection to the Buckeyes and their return to prominence under his watch.

When it comes to what Jim Tressel means to Ohio State fans, the ovation inside of Ohio Stadium in 2012 said everything you need to know.

Urban Meyer vs. Woody Hayes

Urban Meyer's most vivid memories of the Ohio State–Michigan game were born in a shopping plaza.

It was the last week of November in the mid-1970s and Gisela Meyer had an errand to run. Without a babysitter in sight, she grabbed her son and headed to an outdoor mall in Ashtabula.

By that point, Urban was already plenty familiar with the rivalry between the Buckeyes and the Wolverines. But it was at that moment he realized just how special The Game truly was.

"My mother, for some reason I still to this day don't know why, grabbed me and said we have to go run an errand. What the hell we talking about? You don't leave that game," Meyer recalled in 2016. "In Ashtabula, Ohio, outdoor mall walking down, and over the loud speakers I just kept stopping and listening to the game. In the '70s, the Ten Year War. I remember that."

Like most kids in the Buckeye State, Meyer sided with Ohio State and its legendary coach Woody Hayes over Michigan and Hayes' adversary, Bo Schembechler.

"You got beat up in school if you weren't a Buckeye or Woody Hayes guy," Meyer said in 2006, per AlligatorSports.org. "And certainly, I loved him."

More than 40 years after listening to The Game on the loud speakers during a shopping trip with his mother and a decade after his house in Gainesville included a portrait of Hayes, Meyer has now carved his own unique place in the rivalry and goes to work every day in a building named after his childhood idol. And while Tressel's success and adoption of Hayes' motto of "you win with people" may have conjured up memories in Columbus of the Buckeyes' most beloved coach, the remnants of Hayes' trademark intensity are most apparent in Meyer.

In fact, during his time as a grad assistant on Earle Bruce's Ohio State staff, Meyer witnessed Hayes' unique approach firsthand.

"Ohio State had lost the bowl game, so Earl Bruce brings in Woody Hayes. I had been there just a week and I'm thinking, *Holy...this is Coach Hayes*. I'm sitting in the back. Coach Hayes was not healthy at the time, but stands up and starts laying into the coaching staff about toughness," Meyer recalled at the Ohio coaches' convention in 2013. "That we have no toughness in the program. That's why we lost the game. On and on and screaming, this old guy pounding the table. He says, 'We have no toughness, and the reason is because you're not tough. No one on this staff is tough enough, and that's a problem.'"

Hayes didn't stop there.

"He reaches down and grabs this box, slides the top, and there was something in the box moving around," Meyer remembered. "He reaches in and he pulls out this turtle. He reaches down, this turtle's snapping, and he says, 'I'm going to show you toughness.' He unzips his pants and takes out whatever he takes out. The turtle reaches up and snaps at him. You see the veins and the sweat [on Hayes]. He screams at the coaches, 'That's toughness! That's f'n toughness!' He reaches down, pokes the turtle right in the eye, and it falls off. He wipes the sweat off his forehead and says, 'That's the problem. We don't have anybody in this room tough enough to do that right there."

Suffice to say, Woody Hayes did things his own way. It was a common theme throughout a career that would make him a college football coaching legend and the gold standard on the sideline at Ohio State.

A native of the city of Clifton, in southwest Ohio, Wayne Woodrow Hayes starred as a center at Newcomerstown High School before playing tackle for Tom Rogers at Denison University in Granville, Ohio. After his playing career had come to an end, Hayes jumped right into the coaching ranks, serving as an assistant at Mingo Junction High School in east Ohio and New Philadelphia High School.

In 1938, New Philadelphia promoted Hayes—who was then just 25 years old—to its head coaching position following the departure of its former head coach John Brickels. Under the direction of Hayes, the Quakers compiled a 17–2–1 record from 1938 to '39 before falling to 1–9 in his third season as a head coach.

Hayes' coaching career would then take a hiatus as he enlisted the United States Navy in 1941, eventually rising to the rank of lieutenant commander during World War II.

"People talk about how devoted Woody is to football. He was just as dedicated to the Navy," Hayes' wife, Anne, said, per ElevenWarriors .com. "Why, we had been married only five days when he asked for sea duty. He didn't get it at once, but he did request it."

As the war wound down, Hayes eyed a return to coaching and his alma mater just so happened to be looking for a football coach after reinstating its program, which it had suspended during the war. In 1946, Hayes took over as the head coach at Denison.

Hayes lost his first six games in charge of the Big Red, but earned victories over Capital and Wittenberg to close the campaign. That would prove to be the start of a 19-game winning streak, as Denison compiled a 9–0 record in 1947 and 8–0 mark in 1948, winning Ohio Athletic Conference championships in both seasons.

In 1949, Miami (Ohio) University hired Hayes as its head coach. Sid Gillman had just left the school to take the same job at its arch rival, Cincinnati, and would become a personal adversary of Hayes' on both the field and the recruiting trail.

The Redskins would struggle to a 5–4 record in Hayes' first season on the sideline, losing 27–6 to Gillman's Bearcats, but bounced back to win the Mid-American Conference championship in 1950 with a 9–1 record—including a 28–0 shutout of Cincinnati. Miami's big season, which ended with a win in the Salad Bowl over Arizona State, would put Hayes on the coaching map and in 1951, Ohio State set out to find a new head coach after Wes Fesler stepped down due to health concerns.

Following a coaching search that linked the Buckeyes to the likes of Missouri's Don Faurot, assistant Harry Strobel, and even their own former head coach, Paul Brown, Ohio State hired Hayes as its 19th head coach in program history.

"I'm not coming here looking for security," Hayes said upon taking the job. "I came here for the opportunity."

Hayes' high-intensity approach and rigorous practice schedule came as a culture shock to the Buckeyes, who had become accustomed to a more laid-back culture under the direction of Fesler. It also didn't help that there was little he could point to in terms of immediate results.

In Hayes' first three seasons in Columbus, Ohio State compiled a mediocre 16–9–2 record, never finishing higher than No. 3 in the Big Ten standings. As a result, the Buckeyes entered Hayes' fourth season at Ohio State with little expectations in the conference, let alone on a national level.

After entering the season unranked, however, the Buckeyes would soon skyrocket up the polls thanks to wins over No. 18 California, No. 13 Iowa, and No. 2 Wisconsin in the first five weeks of the campaign. By the time Ohio State's year-end game against Michigan came around, the Buckeyes laid claim to an 8–0 record and the nation's top ranking. After a legendary 21–7 win over the Wolverines, which included a crucial goal-line stand and ensuing 99-yard drive, Ohio State clinched its first Big Ten title under Hayes and the right to play for the national championship against Southern California in the Rose Bowl.

On a rainy day in Pasadena, Buckeyes running back Howard "Hopalong" Cassady ran for 92 yards as Ohio State beat the Trojans 20–7 to win Ohio State's first national championship since 1942. The Buckeyes would repeat as conference champions the following year, but fail to successfully defend their national title as Cassady became the third Heisman Trophy winner in program history.

Hayes would win his second national championship in 1957, as Ohio State recorded a 9–1 record and clinched a 10–7 Rose Bowl victory over Oregon with a Don Sutherin fourth-quarter field goal. In 1961, Hayes added a fourth Big Ten championship to his résumé, but the Buckeyes would go on to endure a six-year conference-championship drought from 1962 to '67—the longest such drought in his time in Columbus.

Ohio State, however, would return to national prominence in 1968, thanks to a group of highly touted second-year players dubbed the "Super Sophomores," which included quarterback Rex Kern, defensive back Jack Tatum, defensive lineman Jim Stillwagon, halfback John Brockington, defensive back Mike Sensibaugh, and tight end Jan White.

Entering the season ranked No. 11 in the country, it wouldn't take long for the Buckeyes to make a statement. In the third week of the season, they toppled top-ranked Purdue 13–0, three weeks before beating No. 16 Michigan State. After blowing out No. 4 Michigan 50–14 in its regular season finale, Ohio State clinched its third national title under Hayes with a 27–16 victory over No. 2 USC.

With the bulk of the Buckeyes' roster back for the following year, Hayes appeared to have a burgeoning dynasty on his hands. Hayes would later reveal that he felt his 1969 team was his best Ohio State squad ever and the Buckeyes would continue their winning streak by winning their first eight games of the season.

In Ohio State's ninth game, however, the No. 12 Wolverines would spoil their rival's season, beating the Buckeyes 24–12 in Ann Arbor under the direction of their first-year head coach Bo Schembechler. "Damn you, Bo, you'll never win a bigger game!" was quoted as saying at a banquet years later.

Michigan's victory would spark what would become known as the "Ten Year War" between Hayes and Schembechler, who played offensive tackle for Hayes during his time at Miami. From 1969 to 1978, either the Buckeyes or Wolverines would win shares of each of the next 10 Big Ten championships and combine for 10 Rose Bowl appearances as Michigan held a 5–4–1 record—including wins in their final three contests—over Ohio State in what is widely regarded as college football's greatest rivalry.

There may have never been a fiercer rivalry between too head coaches than the one between Hayes and his former pupil. But despite their public personas, the two shared a deep admiration for one another, a balance between hatred and respect that came to shape the way The Game is viewed.

"There was plenty to criticize about Woody Hayes," Schembechler wrote in his 1989 autobiography with Mitch Albom. "His methods were tough, his temper was, at times, unforgivable. And, unless you knew him or played for him, it is hard to explain why you *liked* being around the guy. But you didn't just like it, you loved it. He was simply fascinating."

Fascinating might also be the best way to describe Hayes' departure from Ohio State.

After losing his third consecutive game against Schembechler, Hayes' 1978 Buckeyes found themselves facing Clemson in the Gator Bowl. Trailing the Tigers 17–15 late in the fourth quarter, Ohio State quarterback Art Schlichter threw an interception to Clemson nose guard Charlie Bauman, who returned the ball toward the Buckeyes sideline before being tackled. As Bauman rose from the ground, Hayes struck him in the throat with an apparent punch, inciting a bench-clearing brawl in the process. The play resulted in not one, but two 15-yard penalties on Ohio State after Hayes went after an official.

The following day, Ohio State fired Hayes.

"Nobody despises to lose more than I do," he said following his firing, per the *New York Times*. "That's got me into trouble over the years, but it also made a man of mediocre ability into a pretty good coach."

In 28 seasons at Ohio State, Hayes amassed a 205–61–10 record, won three consensus national titles, claimed two others (1961, 1970), won 13 Big Ten championships, and produced three Heisman Trophies, including the only two-time winner in the history of the award, Archie Griffin (1974, 1975). In 1983, Hayes was inducted into the College Football Hall of Fame. He passed away after a heart attack in 1987—a day after introducing his rival, Schembechler, at a banquet in Dayton, Ohio.

By any measure, Hayes was undoubtedly one of the greatest and most accomplished coaches in college football history. But as much as he is remembered for accolades, his quirks and anecdotes helped make Hayes the living legend that he was.

Be it his trademark black Block "O" Ohio State hat, his black-rimmed glasses, or his refusal to buy gas across the Michigan border or wear long sleeves—even in the snow—Hayes was every bit a symbol for Ohio State as he was a head coach.

Thus it should come as no surprise that, while growing up an Ohio State fan, it was Hayes whom Urban Meyer idolized most.

"*Fan* is not a strong enough word," Meyer said of Hayes, recalling the brief interactions he shared with his hero during his stint as a Buckeyes graduate assistant in 1986. "To think I admired him, yes, and there's always been a portrait in my house of Coach Hayes...it goes back real thick, real strong and real thick, the admiration I have for Coach Hayes."

Just five years into his Ohio State career, it's too early to compare Meyer's legacy to Hayes', but already, similarities are apparent. Like his idol, Meyer has placed an increased emphasis on the Buckeyes' rivalry with Michigan, referring to the Wolverines as only "That Team Up North" and requiring push-ups for any of his players who dare utter the "M" word.

Meyer's even had his own "super sophomores," as his first national title at Ohio State came in large part thanks to the play of second-year players like Ezekiel Elliott, Joey Bosa, Darron Lee, Eli Apple, Vonn Bell, and Jalin Marshall.

One of the original super sophomores, Kern has seen the comparisons between his former head coach and Ohio State's current one and doesn't seem to think they're all that out of line.

"The intensity and passion are there," Kern told *Sporting News* in 2015 after the Buckeyes captured the College Football Playoff championship.

"The comments Urban made afterward, 'This is for the great state of Ohio, for the great university of Ohio State; it's for the football program, but it's also for the players.' That hit home."

Over the course of his career, Meyer already possesses as many outright national championships as Hayes, but trails him in conference titles, All-Americans, Heisman Trophy winners, and total wins. With 238 total victories over the course of his entire head coaching career, Hayes ranks No. 14 all-time among Division I head coaches.

Meyer, of course, has made plenty of history of his own, and his career winning percentage of .851 trumps Hayes' mark of .761 and ranks sixth all-time and tops among active head coaches. As he enters his 16th season as a head coach, it's unlikely Meyer's longevity will ever match that of Hayes, although with Jim Harbaugh's arrival in Ann Arbor, many have already speculated that a second edition of the Ten Year War might already be upon us.

If that's the case, Meyer's already off to a 2–0 head start and 5–0 overall advantage in the rivalry he grew up revering—a rivalry he understands the importance of thanks to the man whose statue he passes every day on his way into the Ohio State football facility that bears Hayes' name.

"I appreciate rivalries probably more than most. That's just the way I've always been," Meyer said in 2016. "I think that came from Coach Hayes and Bo Schembechler. I just think that was the classiest—both programs had a tremendous respect for each other, both coaches did, and they played so damn hard."

Considering the two coaches who were on their respective sidelines, the Buckeyes and Wolverines never had much of a choice.

★ ★ ★

Urban Meyer vs. Bo Schembechler

Shortly after accepting the offer to become Bowling Green's next head coach, Urban Meyer received a call from one of the school's most famous alums.

Thirteen years prior, Meyer was serving as a graduate assistant on Earle Bruce's final Ohio State staff when he ventured from the locker room and into the hallway prior to what would be his boss' final game as the Buckeyes' head coach. There, Meyer found himself standing mere inches away from one of his coaching idols.

"I happened to be the guy at the door, I was just a G.A. so I had no impact—I was just a guy that made coffee—and coach Bruce says a few words to the team and it is freezing cold and I opened the tunnel doors, and their locker room's right across," Meyer said. "There's standing Bo Schembechler and a bunch of big players right behind him. I just remember I turned around — you know here's a guy who grew up with the rivalry, 21 years old. I just kind of froze.

"I'm six feet away from coach Schembechler and I remember that very well. I mean, it was one of those moments."

Thirteen years later, Meyer found himself in the midst of a similar moment on the line with Schembechler, who had served as an assistant coach at Meyer's new school in 1955.

"Bo Schembechler called me when I got the Bowling Green job," Meyer recalled to ESPN's Mark Schlabach in 2015. "He told me, 'I know you're one of Earle's guys. It's good to see one of his guys doing well.'"

For Meyer, the moment served as a surreal welcome to the head coaching ranks from a head coach he grew up both idolizing and rooting against in the Ten Year War. And although Meyer has always been attached to the opposite side of the rivalry, Schembechler is best remembered for, his respect for The Game has been strongly shaped by the legendary Michigan head coach's impact on it.

"You're darn right it was tough," Meyer said of Schembechler's rivalry with Woody Hayes. "But I know very well that there are two coaches who never respected each other more, and that's the head coach of our rival, Bo Schembechler, because I talked to him about it. I had great conversations with Coach Schembechler."

There might not be a figure more associated with college football's most storied rivalry—and the one Meyer's now a part of—than the former Wolverines head coach.

A native of Barberton, Ohio, just outside of Akron, Schembechler's rise through the coaching ranks wasn't just embedded in The Game, but also both sides of it.

After starring as an offensive tackle at Barberton High School, Schembechler accepted a scholarship to spend his college career at Miami (Ohio). There, he spent his first three seasons playing under legendary head coach Sid Gillman, who is credited with laying the foundation for what would later become the West Coast offense.

After the Redskins compiled a 9–0–1 record, including a win in the Sun Bowl, in Schembechler's junior season in 1948, Gillman departed for Miami's rival, Cincinnati. His replacement would be Hayes, whose more hard-nosed approach appealed to Schembechler, who served as one of the Redskins' captains in Hayes' first season in Oxford.

Miami went 5–4 in Schembechler's senior season and two years later he would reunite with Hayes as a graduate assistant in Columbus after his former head coach took over at Ohio State. After his first season with the Buckeyes, Schembechler would spend two years on a tour with the U.S. Army, before returning to the coaching ranks as a member of Bill Crutchfield's first staff at Presbyterian in 1954.

In 1955, Schembechler headed to Bowling Green, but would only spend one season coaching the Falcons freshmen. In 1957, he joined Ara Parseghian's—whom he had coached alongside at Miami—staff at Northwestern, where he served as the defensive coordinator.

After two seasons in Evanston, Schembechler returned to Columbus, once again reuniting with Hayes as an Ohio State assistant. Over the course of five seasons with the Buckeyes, Schembechler became one of Hayes' closest allies and most trusted assistants.

"I have a lot of friends there. I coached there for six years. There are guys there that are really close friends of mine," Schembechler recalled in 2006. "I never brought it up when I coached, but I have close ties at Ohio State. Unfortunately, I even have a graduate degree from there. They made me go to school while I was a graduate assistant."

Over the course of his career in Columbus, he even developed a new dream—to become his mentor's successor as Ohio State's head coach. So when his alma mater, Miami, offered him its head coaching position in 1963, Schembechler accepted in hopes of bolstering his coaching résumé—much to Hayes' chagrin.

"That was my goal in life, to replace Woody Hayes. Absolutely, that's what I wanted," Schembechler told Michigan's official website in 2006. "I went down to Miami, and [Ohio State athletic director] Dick Larkins told me, 'You'd better win down there if you go.' That's what he said. I said, 'Okay.'

"I went down there, and Woody told me I'd be foolish to go, because I would be the next coach at Ohio State. I said, 'Well, geez, how much longer are you going to coach?' He said, 'Oh, four or five years, probably.'

As it would turn out, Hayes would wind up coaching Ohio State for another 15 years. Nevertheless, Schembechler's return to Oxford, where he compiled a 40–17–3 record over the course of six seasons and won shares of two Mid-American Conference championships, proved worthwhile.

In 1969, Michigan hired Schembechler to become its 15th head coach in program history following an interview process that lasted all of 15 minutes.

"His personality just struck me right away," U-M athletic director Don Canham told the *Michigan Daily* in 2004. "I hired him 15 minutes after we began to talk. That was the turning point in my career as athletic director."

It didn't take long for Canham's gamble to payoff.

In Schembechler's first season in Ann Arbor, the Wolverines compiled an 8–3 record, with a win over rival and defending champion Ohio State clinching their first Big Ten championship and Rose Bowl appearance in five seasons. Michigan's upset over the Buckeyes would also jumpstart what would come to be known as the Ten Year War between Schembechler and Hayes, a decade-long stretch in which the two programs combined to win at least a share of every conference championship.

In Schembechler's second season with the Wolverines, Michigan won its first eight contests, but had its championship quest spoiled by Ohio State. In what was a top-five matchup between the two programs, the Buckeyes beat the Wolverines 20–9 in Columbus, punching their own ticket to Pasadena—and a claimed national title—in the process.

From 1971 to '74, Michigan compiled a 41–3–1 record, never winning fewer than 10 games or losing more than once in a single season. But while the Wolverines won shares of four consecutive Big Ten championships over that span, a 1–2–1 record against Hayes' Buckeyes prevented U-M from winning a national title over that four-year stretch.

In what would become one of the most historic editions of The Game, Ohio State and Michigan played to a 10–10 tie in 1973, marking the completion of a 10–0–1 season for the Wolverines—their first undefeated campaign since 1948. But with the top-ranked Buckeyes also laying claim to an undefeated record, the two teams split the conference title, leaving the Big Ten athletic directors to vote on which team would represent the league in the Rose Bowl with a potential national championship on the line.

Ohio State would win the vote 6–4, due in large part to a broken collarbone suffered by Wolverines quarterback Dennis Franklin. The loss—and subsequent controversial vote—stuck with Schembechler until his final days.

"It was the greatest disappointment of my career," he said in 2006. "We were both undefeated. We came in undefeated and we were playing here, and we missed a field goal at the end and we end up tied. It was a 10–10 tie. Everybody, including Woody Hayes, congratulated me after the game and said, oh, you'll do a great job in the Rose Bowl and all that. And everybody expected Michigan to go to the Rose Bowl. Because if you look at the game, we outplayed them. If you look at tradition, Ohio State had played in the Rose Bowl the year before, and we used to have a no-repeat rule where you couldn't repeat.

"So everything indicated that we were going to go to the Rose Bowl. And it was strictly a political thing. And I assume the fact that our great quarterback, Dennis Franklin, broke his collarbone in the fourth quarter of that game on a blitz, that they might have used that as an excuse."

After consecutive losses to Ohio State in 1974 and 1975, Schembechler would go on to win the final three games of the Ten Year War, winning his seventh, eighth, and ninth Big Ten championships from 1976 to '78.

Schembechler's run of success would continue through the 1980s and it wouldn't be until his 15th season in Ann Arbor that he would fail to post a winning record, as the 1984 Wolverines went 6–6 after sophomore starting quarterback Jim Harbaugh broke his arm early in the season.

By the time he opted to retire at the end of the 1989 campaign at the age of 60, Schembechler had recorded a career record of 194–48–5, having earned shares of 13 Big Ten championships, a record that still stands—while tied with Hayes—for the most ever by a league coach.

More so than his numbers, however, Schembechler is best remembered for helping shape what would become the modern era of the Michigan football. And ironically, it all started back in his first season in Ann Arbor—and with heavy influence from his mentor-turned-rival.

Looking to instill a Hayes-like toughness in the Wolverines, Schembechler warned of a dramatic culture change that was coming to the U-M program. In 1969, Schembechler saw his 140-man roster nearly cut in half to 75 following a grueling training camp with rigorous conditioning.

All along the way, Schembechler issued a promise that doubled as a rallying cry: "Those who stay will be champions." It still serves as a signature slogan in the Wolverines program today.

From 1990 to '92, Schembechler served as the president of the Detroit Tigers baseball team. He also remained close to Michigan throughout the duration of his life and maintained an office at the Wolverines football facility—Schembechler Hall—as he was succeeded by two of his assistant coaches in Gary Moeller (1990–1994) and Lloyd Carr (1995–2007).

Schembechler passed away due to heart disease on November 17, 2006—two days before No. 2 Michigan faced No. 1 Ohio State in the most highly anticipated edition of The Game since the Ten Year War. A day earlier, he had delivered his traditional pregame pep talk to the Wolverines.

By any measure, Schembechler is one of the most accomplished and iconic coaches in college football history. His 234 career wins are good for the 38th most all-time and his .775 winning percentage ranks 20th in college football history.

The lone blemish on his coaching résumé stems from having never won a national championship in his 27 years as a head coach. For that reason, any coaching pantheon would have to have Schembechler a tier lower than Meyer, whose 10–3 mark in bowl games also stands as significantly more impressive than Schembechler's 5–12 record in postseason play.

Ultimately, the respective eras they coached in make Meyer's and Schembechler's legacies difficult to measure against one another.

What is comparable, however, is the impact each has made on not just the game of college football, but The Game they both grew up with, as evidenced by the reverence toward Schembechler that Meyer still shows when he speaks of him to this day.

"There's a mutual respect," Meyer said of Schembechler and Hayes. "And I learned it from those two—two of the greatest coaches of all time. They handled themselves with incredible class, toughness, demanded of their players, and you got to see that every time those two teams played. So that's my memory, and that's how we go about our business here."

Urban Meyer vs. Joe Paterno

Hanging in Urban Meyer's Ohio State office is a picture from the most forgettable season of his coaching career.

No, the photo from the 2011 Outback Bowl that sits on Meyer's shelf isn't there as a source of motivation, a reminder that even when your program appears to be on track, an unmemorable 8–5 campaign could be around the corner, as was the case for Florida in 2010. Nor is it a tribute to his time in Gainesville, as the snapshot depicts his final time walking across the sideline after a game as the Gators' head coach.

Rather, what makes the picture of Meyer in his blue-and-orange windbreaker stand out from the other photos that line his shelf is whom he's standing alongside, as the Buckeyes head coach has never been shy to share his affection for former Penn State coach Joe Paterno.

"I've said that thousands of times, and I don't mind saying it again because I love the man. I consider him one of my closest friends and allies in this game of college football," Meyer said in his Outback Bowl press conference, after his Florida team beat Paterno's Nittany Lions 37–24. "You just get tired of hearing about the bad. Joe Paterno is about the good. There's a time in life you just like to talk about the good. When you talk about good in college football, Joe Paterno's name is at the top of the list."

For the better part of four decades, Meyer's comments were held by most as a common belief. Paterno's iconic presence was often cited as a bright spot in college football, a symbol for all that was still right in the sport.

Unfortunately, mere months after meeting Meyer in the Outback Bowl, Paterno's time in State College would come to an unceremonious end as a result of the Jerry Sandusky child-abuse scandal that rocked Penn State to its core. But even after Paterno's passing in early 2012 was clouded in controversy regarding how much blame he deserved for the apparent wrongdoing that had occurred under his watch, Meyer stood by his former friend and what he believed he had stood for.

"I think he is the model of compliance, he is the model for academic performance and demanding achievement by his players, and I don't think those things will ever be matched," Meyer told the Cleveland *Plain Dealer* following Paterno's death.

In the time since Paterno's passing, the legacy of the longtime Nittany Lions head coach has become one of the most polarizing subjects in all of college football.

What isn't debatable, however, is the impact Paterno had on the sport over the course of a career unlike any other in its history.

A native of Brooklyn, New York, Paterno was born in 1926 to Italian immigrants Florence de LaSalle and Angelo Lafayette Paterno. After graduating from high school, he spent a year in the U.S. Army during World War II before attending Brown University, where he played quarterback and cornerback for the Bears.

In his three years of action in Providence, Brown compiled a 19–7–1 record, including an 8–1 campaign in his senior season. Over the course of his career, Paterno recorded 14 interceptions as a defensive player, a school record that still stands today and has since been tied by Greg Parker (1993–1996).

Paterno's starring role, however, came as the lead man in the Bears' Wing-T offense.

"He was like having another coach on the field," his head coach, Rip Engle, said in 1949, per the Penn State website. "I've coached better runners and better passers, but I've never coached a more heady quarterback."

After graduating from Brown with a degree in English, Paterno briefly considered attending Boston University's School of Law. But when Engle left to become the head coach at Penn State, Paterno went with him, joining the Nittany Lions' staff as an assistant coach in 1950.

It would mark the first and final stop of Paterno's coaching career.

Engle enjoyed a lengthy 16-year stint in charge of the Penn State program, compiling an impressive 104–48–4 record from 1950 to '65.

Over the course of that span, the Nittany Lions laid claim to seven top-20 finishes and a 3–1 record in bowl games.

Following a 7–3 campaign in 1963, Engle promoted Paterno to associate head coach. And after Engle retired following a 5–5 season in 1965, Paterno was named his successor.

Paterno inherited a program that struggled to maintain consistency over the course of its first 78 years of existence. By the time Paterno was named head coach, Penn State had already possessed 13 head coaches, only three of whom had lasted more than five seasons. Engle's tenure had by far been the most fruitful in program history, but his success had slipped in his final seasons as the Nittany Lions compiled an 18–12 record from 1963 to '65.

In Paterno's debut season, the mediocrity would continue as Penn State recorded its second straight 5–5 record in 1966. The Nittany Lions would get off to a rough start in Paterno's second season in charge in Happy Valley as well, losing two of their first three games, including a 17–15 defeat at the hands of No. 4 UCLA.

Bigger and better things for the Penn State program, however, would soon arrive.

After its 1–2 start to the 1967 campaign, the Nittany Lions went on to win their next seven games, including a 13–8 victory over No. 3 North Carolina State. After tying Florida State in the Gator Bowl, Penn State would finish the season ranked No. 10 in the AP Top 25, the program's second top-10 finish in the previous 20 years.

The following season, the Nittany Lions would record their first undefeated, untied record in school history, winning all 11 of their games including a victory over No. 6 Kansas in the Orange Bowl. Despite its perfect record, Penn State would finish second in the AP Top 25 as Woody Hayes' Ohio State and its super sophomores were proclaimed national champions. The Nittany Lions would find themselves in the same predicament a year later, once again winning all of 11 of their games but finishing second behind Texas in both the AP and Coaches polls.

Despite having yet to have won a national championship, Paterno had his version of the Penn State program rolling. In 1973, he would add a third perfect season in eight years to his résumé as running back John Cappelletti became the first Heisman Trophy winner in school history. A national championship, however, would remain elusive to the Nittany Lions, who finished the 1973 campaign ranked No. 5 in both major polls, with just two wins—vs. No. 20 Pittsburgh and No. 13 LSU—against ranked opponents to their credit.

"To be frank," Paterno said, per the *New York Times*, "I feel those three teams (1968, 1969, and 1973) each deserved to be No. 1. Those three teams had as much right to be No. 1 those years as anybody else."

In what was considered a golden age of college football, Penn State found itself keeping pace with the likes of Hayes' Ohio State, Bear Bryant's Alabama, Barry Switzer's Oklahoma, and Bo Schembechler's Michigan. In his first full decade as a head coach in the 1970s, Paterno compiled a record of 96–22, only failing to finish a season ranked once, including six top-10 finishes.

Paterno's momentum would carry into the 1980s, as the Nittany Lions opened the decade with back-to-back 10–2 seasons, finishing the 1981 season ranked No. 3 in both major polls.

In 1982, Penn State would open the year ranked No. 8 in the AP Top 25 and rose all the way to No. 3 before falling to No. 4 Alabama 42–21 in Birmingham. Despite the lopsided defeat, the Nittany Lions rallied to win their final seven games, including a 27–23 victory over top-ranked Georgia in the Sugar Bowl.

With an 11–1 record and a résumé that included wins against five ranked opponents, including the nation's No. 1 team at year's end, Penn

State finished the season ranked first in both major polls, giving the Nittany Lions their first national championship in program history.

"There is no question in my mind we are the No. 1 team," Paterno said per the *New York Times*, among controversy that 11–0–1 SMU had finished second in the polls. "This is the best team we have had at Penn State."

It wouldn't take long for the 1982 Nittany Lions to find company in that discussion.

After a bid for a second national championship fell short as Penn State compiled an 11–0 record before losing to Oklahoma in the Orange Bowl in 1985, the Nittany Lions entered the 1986 season ranked No. 6 in the country. Thanks to a dominant defense that held eight opponents to 15 points or fewer—including No. 2 Alabama to just three points in a 23–3 Penn State victory in Tuscaloosa—the Nittany Lions rose to second in the polls heading into a Fiesta Bowl matchup against No. 1 Miami (Florida).

In what was dubbed as "the Duel in the Desert," the Penn State defense intercepted Hurricanes Heisman Trophy–winning quarterback Vinny Testaverde five times—the final one coming in the end zone in the final seconds of action—to secure a 14–10 victory and the Nittany Lions' second national championship of the Paterno era.

That same year, *Sports Illustrated* named Paterno its 1986 Sportsman of the Year. Now 20 years into his head coaching career, the man the people in Happy Valley referred to as "Joe Pa" was a living legend.

"In an era of college football in which it seems everybody's hand is either in the till or balled up in a fist, Paterno sticks out like a clean thumb. His standard of excellence is so season-in, season-out consistent it borders on the monotonous: win 10, 11 games; send off another bunch of future doctors, lawyers and accountants," Rick Reilly wrote in his cover-story profile, "Not an Ordinary Joe." "Over the last three decades, nobody has stayed truer to the game and at the same time truer to himself than Joseph Vincent Paterno."

Paterno's success would continue into the 1990s, even as his program found itself in the midst of transition. After maintaining its independence for the first 105 years of its existence, Penn State joined the Big Ten conference at the start of the 1993 season.

In their debut campaign in the league, the Nittany Lions posted an impressive 10–2 record, losing only to traditional Big Ten powers Ohio State and Michigan. Any questions about Penn State's viability with the top end of the conference, however, would be quelled a season later, as the Nittany Lions won their first 11 games—including a 63–14 beatdown of the Buckeyes—and represented the conference as the Big Ten champion in the Rose Bowl.

Only a win over No. 12 Oregon in Pasadena wouldn't be enough for Penn State to pass top-ranked Nebraska in the final polls of the 1994 season. It would mark the fifth undefeated record of Paterno's coaching career—and the fourth time such a season didn't result in a national title.

Throughout the remainder of the 1990s, the Nittany Lions never lost more than three games in a single season, finishing every year from 1989 to 1999 ranked, including five top-five finishes. In 2001, Beaver Stadium expanded its capacity from 93,967 to more than 107,000, making it the second-largest college football stadium in the country—an indicator of the prominence of the Penn State brand.

The Nittany Lions' success, however, began to slip at the turn of the new millennium as Paterno failed to replicate his success of the previous decades upon entering his 70s. In 2000, Penn State recorded a 5–7 record, its first losing mark since 1988 and only its second under Paterno's watch. The Nittany Lions' struggles continued into 2001 as they got off to an 0–4 start to the season before finishing the year with a 5–6 record.

Penn State would briefly bounce back to a 9–4 record and top-15 finish in 2002, before falling to 3–9 in 2003 and 4–7 in 2004—its two worst seasons of the Paterno era. Yet despite diminishing results and a head coach now approaching his 80s, the Nittany Lions managed to keep pace on the recruiting trail, routinely signing top-25 nationally ranked classes into the 2000s, including the country's No. 7 class in 2006 and No. 12 class in 2010.

Amid rumors of Paterno's impending retirement, Penn State won a share of its second Big Ten championship in 2005, tallying an 11–1 record including a triple-overtime victory over Florida State and its own legendary head coach, Bobby Bowden, in the Orange Bowl before finishing the season ranked No. 3 behind BCS champion Texas and runner-up USC. Paterno would win his third Big Ten championship in 2008, as the Nittany Lions recorded an 11–1 regular season before falling to USC in the Rose Bowl at the end of the year.

After posting a second consecutive 11–2 record in 2009, which included a victory over LSU in the Capital One Bowl, Penn State fell to 7–6 in 2010 before getting off to an 8–1 start through its first nine games of the 2011 season.

With his team firmly in contention for another conference title and ranked No. 12 in the country, Paterno wouldn't be allowed to stick around and see the rest of the season through. After reports of a child abuse scandal involving Paterno's longtime defensive coordinator, Jerry Sandusky, rocked the college football world, Paterno announced he would retire at season's end. The Penn State Board of Trustees, however, would reject Paterno's offer and fired the 46th-year head coach, alongside school president Graham Spanier.

Paterno passed away less than three months later following a brief bout with lung cancer.

Sandusky, who served as a Penn State assistant under Paterno from 1969 to 1999, was arrested and eventually found guilty of 45 charges pertaining to the sexual abuse of multiple young boys. A report performed by former FBI director Louis Freeh and commissioned by the Penn State Board of Trustees later found that multiple "powerful leaders" at the school—including Paterno—"repeatedly concealed critical facts relating to Sandusky's child abuse from authorities, the University's Board of Trustees, the Penn State community, and at large."

The accusations had spanned over the course of Sandusky's final five seasons as the Nittany Lions' defensive coordinator (1994–1999) and well into the following decade following his sudden retirement, in which he remained in close contact with the Penn State program. While the findings of the Freeh report have been largely disputed, accusations that Paterno had been aware of Sandusky's crimes and failed to properly report them now date back to 1976.

In 2012, then-68-year-old Sandusky was sentenced to 30 to 60 years in prison. Penn State, meanwhile, received the harshest sanctions in NCAA history, including a four-year bowl ban and the loss of 40 scholarships, although the punishment was ultimately lessened in 2014, with the bowl ban cut short and scholarships later fully restored. Initially, Paterno and Penn State's records from 1998 to 2011 had been vacated as well, although the 112 victories were restored in 2015.

With the restoration, Paterno's career record stands at 409–136–3—giving him the most wins by a coach in Division I college football history. He also lays claim to the most bowl appearances (37) and bowl victories (24) in the history of the sport.

Although his reputation and legacy have been the subject of debate since his firing in 2011 and subsequent passing, it's indisputable that based on his on-field accomplishments, Paterno is one of the greatest coaches in college football history.

In addition to his 409 victories and two national championships, Paterno's five perfect seasons tie him with Bernie Bierman and Knute Rockne for the third most in the history of the sport. Over the course of his 46 seasons on the State College sidelines, Penn State produced 251 NFL draft picks and another 100 players who signed NFL contracts, including some of professional football's most prominent players in linebacker Jack Ham, guard Mike Munchak, running back Franco Harris, linebacker Matt Millen, defensive end Tamba Hali, and running back Larry Johnson.

For comparison's sake, in his first 15 seasons as a college head coach, Meyer has amassed 165 victories and produced 61 NFL draft picks. At his current winning percentage of .851—which tops Paterno's mark of .749—it would take Meyer nearly 22 more 13-game seasons to catch up to his idol. Suffice to say, that likely isn't happening.

"I've known coach Paterno longer than he's known me," Meyer said in the days leading up to their Outback Bowl battle. "And I was fortunate I was born with great coaches in that era, always had great admiration for how they ran programs."

Ultimately, the Paterno's unprecedented longevity and the respective eras in which both Meyer and Paterno coached make their legacies difficult to compare. While Meyer has already won one more national title in a career that's lasted just barely a third of Paterno's, the majority of the Penn State legend's time on the sideline was spent during an era in which voters possessed the most power when it came to determining national titles.

Yet regardless of how their respective résumés stack up, what was an otherwise meaningless bowl game at the end of the 2010 campaign made this much clear: the respect that Meyer and Paterno—two of the best ever in their profession—share for each other is immense.

"He's a big, good-looking guy. He's a really good family man. He's got a lot of things he can do," Paterno said of Meyer and his departure from Florida at the time. "He's making some decisions which I'm sure are not easy for him, but he's making them. I admire him and respect him for what he's doing."

Added Meyer of Paterno: "He will go down as the greatest football coach in the history of the game. Every young coach, in my opinion, can take a lesson from him."

PART IV

★ ★ ★

Urban Meyer: Legacy

By the Numbers

Over the course of the first 15 years of his head coaching career, Urban Meyer has reached several notable milestones and compiled a bevy of impressive accomplishments.

And although it's difficult to define one's legacy based only on numbers, from a statistical standpoint, Meyer's career more than stands on its own.

What follows is a look at the numbers that tell the story of where Meyer stacks up in the college football coaching pantheon and some context to the digits that define his unique place in the sport's history.

.851

Arguably the most impressive number on Meyer's résumé, his .851 winning percentage is good for the fourth best in college football history among Division-I head coaches. It also stands as the highest winning percentage among active Division I head coaches with Washington's Chris Petersen and his .817 winning percentage being next in line.

Meyer's teams have won more than 90 percent of their games seven times in his coaching career. Only twice have they ever failed to top 70.

For comparison's sake, his winning percentage tops coaching legends Barry Switzer (.837), Tom Osborne (.836), Fielding Yost (.833), Bear Bryant (.780), Bo Schembechler (.775), and Woody Hayes (.759). It also tops current coaching contemporaries Bob Stoops (.796), Nick Saban (.760), Gary Patterson (.753), and Mark Richt (.740).

Fifteen seasons in, Meyer's career has already outlasted the three Division I head coaches with higher winning percentages than his, meaning no coach in history has matched the longevity of his sustained success. Those three coaches—Knute Rockne (.881), Frank Leahy (.864), and Doyt Perry (.855)—have each already been inducted into the College Football Hall of Fame.

It likely won't be long until Meyer joins them.

3

When Ohio State won the inaugural College Football Playoff Meyer entered rarefied air, as he became one of 15 coaches in the sport's history to lay claim to three national championships. Of those 15 coaches, Meyer is one of four to have won at least one of his titles post-1980.

While the polls era that predated made national champions tougher to decipher—for example, both Hayes and Texas' Darrell Royal lay claim to the 1970 crown—only Saban has found as much success as Meyer in the BCS era and beyond. Following the implementation of the BCS in 1998, Meyer and Saban are the only head coaches to have won multiple outright national championships and the two were the first to win College Football Playoff championships as well.

With three national championships to his credit, Meyer still trails John McKay (4), Leahy (4), Saban (5), Howard Jones (5), Hayes (5), Bernie Bierman (5), and Bear Bryant (6) in terms of claimed titles.

But when it comes to the modern era, only Saban has matched Meyer's success.

26–3

Over the course of his career, Meyer has never been shy to place a heavy emphasis on rivalry games—and for good reason. In his 15 years as a head coach, Meyer's teams are 26–3 in contests against their chief rivals.

That record includes Meyer's 1–1 record vs. Toledo during his time at Bowling Green; a 4–0 mark vs. both Utah State and BYU at Utah;a combined 16–2 record against Georgia, Tennessee, and Florida State at Florida; and a perfect mark against Michigan in his first five years as Ohio State's head coach.

You'd be hard pressed to find a head coach in college football history more dominant in rivalry games than Meyer's been. In his time at Michigan State, LSU, and Alabama, Saban is 18–10 against his team's rivals and Stoops is 11–7 against Texas in his first 18 years as Oklahoma's head coach.

The most apt comparison might be Jim Tressel, who laid claim to an impressive 9–1 record against Michigan in his decade at the helm of Ohio State. There's also Pete Carroll, whose USC teams went 8–1 against UCLA in his nine seasons with the Trojans.

From a statistical standpoint, Meyer also benefits from the fact that at Florida, he faced three rivals on an annual basis. But it doesn't take much more than a look at the numbers to realize that he's also made a habit of rising to such occasions.

10–3

Unsurprisingly, Meyer's been just at dominant in the postseason as he has in the regular season. Counting Ohio State's two wins in the College Football Playoff at the end of the 2014 season, Meyer lays claim to a 10–3 record in bowl games.

That puts Meyer ninth all-time in terms of bowl wins, falling one short of Saban, whose career mark stands at 11–9. It's highly unlikely Meyer ever catches up to Joe Paterno's 24 bowl victories or Bobby Bowden's 22, but it's not unreasonable to think—especially in the playoff era—that when Meyer's career is done, he could match Bear Bryant's 15 bowl wins, which would currently tie Meyer for the third most all-time.

Even when it comes to the consistency with which Meyer's teams have become bowl eligible, his track record remains remarkable. Since taking over Utah in 2004, only once has one of Meyer's seasons not ended in postseason play—2012, when the Buckeyes team he inherited had been slapped with a bowl ban.

As far as conference championship games are concerned, Meyer lays claim to a 3–2 record, including a 2–1 record in the SEC Championship Game and a 1–1 mark when playing for the Big Ten title.

Regardless of the outcome of those games, however, it's not often Meyer's season has ended in a loss. In 15 years, it's only happened four times.

11

Although Meyer's track record as a coach speaks for itself, he's often the first to deflect any credit he receives to the players he's coached. And with 11 consensus All-Americans to his credit, Meyer has coached some of the best of the very best.

Eleven players in a 15-year span may not seem like a lot, until you consider that in order to be considered a consensus All-American, a player must be named an All-American by at least three of the five following outlets: the Associated Press, the American Football Coaches of America, the Football Writers Association of America, *Sporting News*, and the Walter Camp Football Foundation.

Meyer's first consensus All-American came in 2006, when safety Reggie Nelson earned such honors. By the time he left Gainesville, Tim Tebow, Brandon Spikes, Brandon James, Joe Haden, Maurkice Pouncey, and Chas Henry had each followed suit.

In 2014, Joey Bosa became Meyer's first consensus All-American at Ohio State, an honor he'd repeat in 2015. That same year, offensive tackle

Taylor Decker was selected as a consensus All-American, as were safety Malik Hooker and center Pat Elflein in 2016.

While Saban has set the standard with 30 consensus All-Americans over the span of his career, Meyer's total of 11 trumps coaching contemporaries such as Dabo Swinney (6), Jim Harbaugh (5), and Les Miles (9). And although Meyer trails the likes of Stoops (19) and Jimbo Fisher (12), at the rate he's currently recruiting, it shouldn't take long for the Ohio State head coach to add to his list.

9

When it comes to recruiting rankings, Meyer has maintained a philosophy consistent with his competitive nature: If you're keeping score, we want to win.

On the recruiting trail, Meyer's programs have won more than most.

Dating back to his arrival at Florida and the rise of the online recruiting industry, Meyer has signed nine top-five nationally ranked classes—including the nation's No. 1 class in 2007, according to Rivals.com. Since arriving at Ohio State, five of Meyer's first six classes have ranked in the nation's top five, including four top-three nationally ranked classes.

From 2006 to 2017, only one of Meyer's classes has ranked outside the nation's top 10 as his 2009 Florida haul measured in at No. 11 in the nation. Over that span, the only coach to have achieved similar results on the recruiting trail has been Saban, who has signed each of the nation's seven previous No. 1 classes at Alabama from 2011 to 2017.

Since arriving at Ohio State in 2012, Meyer has signed the top-ranked Big Ten class in each of the past six recruiting cycles. And yet despite only signing 21 prospects—a relatively low number in today's day and age of recruiting—Meyer's 2017 class possessed the highest player rating average in the history of recruiting service 247Sports.com.

Meyer's highly touted hauls have included five-star prospects such as Percy Harvin, Tim Tebow, Carlos Dunlap, Will Hill, Noah Spence, Vonn Bell, Raekwon McMillan, Nick Bosa, Chase Young, and Jeffrey Okudah.

But Meyer hasn't just been successful when it's come to attracting talent. He also has a track record of developing it.

61

While most coaches would prefer their players still around for full years, Meyer has never been shy about encouraging his players to chase their NFL dreams. And over the course of his 15-year head coaching career, Meyer certainly has developed a propensity for putting players in the pros.

Among his time at Bowling Green, Utah, Florida, and Ohio State, Meyer's programs have developed a combined 61 draft picks between the 2002 and 2016 NFL drafts. In 2016, Meyer produced his best draft class yet, as 12 Ohio State players were picked in the draft's first four rounds—a modern draft record. That group included five Buckeyes who selected in the draft's first round, including two players—Joey Bosa and Ezekiel Elliott—picked in the first four picks.

Heading into the 2017 NFL draft, where Ohio State was expected to produce at least six more draft picks, Meyer's 61 players picked ranked fourth among active coaches, trailing only Saban (95), Richt (84), and Stoops (81). When it comes to first-round selections, Meyer laid claim to 16 over the course of his career heading into the 2017 draft—second only behind Saban's 23 among active coaches.

From a historical perspective, Meyer also trails coaches such as Paterno (251), Bowden (182), Mack Brown (101), Steve Spurrier (103), and Frank Beamer (96) in terms of total picks. His pipeline to the pros, however, isn't showing signs of slowing down anytime soon.

165

Entering the 2017 season with a career record of 165–29, Meyer lays claim to the 45th most wins for a Division I head coach in college football history. Should he continue winning at his current rate, it will take fewer than four seasons for Meyer to become what is currently fewer than 20 head coaches in the history of the sport to compile 200 career wins.

Among active coaches, Meyer's 165 victories trails only Saban (205, adjusted from 210), Bill Snyder (202), and Stoops (190). The historic success that Meyer is currently closing in on shouldn't come as much of a surprise. In 2010, he became the sixth-fastest coach to reach 100 career wins and in 2016, he surpassed Bob Stoops' mark of 160 for the most wins ever for a Division I college head coach in the first 15 years of his career.

Depending on how long he continues coaching, it's possible Meyer could crack the all-time top-10 wins list, a spot currently led by Frank Beamer and Mack Brown, each of whom compiled 238 wins over the span of his career.

As it currently stands, Meyer is climbing the wins chart at a historic pace and isn't showing signs of stopping anytime soon. When you factor in all he has already accomplished and the potential of what lies ahead, Meyer's case for being considered the greatest coach in college football history only figures to grow stronger in the coming years.

★ ★ ★

Coaching Tree

On November 27, 2016, Tom Herman stepped to a podium in Austin, Texas, wearing a burnt-orange tie and Longhorns lapel.

Two years earlier, he was still Ohio State's offensive coordinator, helping the Buckeyes navigate their run to the College Football Playoff behind the play of their third-string quarterback.

Now he was the head coach at the University of Texas. And the former Houston head coach's unprecedented ascension up the coaching ranks wouldn't have been possible without the help of his former boss.

"[Working] for Coach Meyer, I feel like I went to head coaching school for three years," Herman said.

He's not alone. Even before he arrived at Ohio State in late 2011, Meyer had already amassed one of the most impressive coaching trees in college football.

It started at Bowling Green, where Meyer's first staff as a head coach included three future head coaches as well as a fourth in a then–graduate assistant named D.J. Durkin. Fifteen years later, Durkin would take over as the head coach at Maryland, where he faced Meyer and the Buckeyes in an early-November matchup.

"It was hard work, [but] it was very enjoyable," Durkin said in the days leading up to his showdown with his former boss, who he also worked for at Florida as a linebackers coach and special teams coordinator in 2010. "I learned a lot from it. A lot of things I learned then are still things that are a major part of my philosophy and what I believe in today."

The same rings true of Meyer's offensive coordinator at Bowling Green, Gregg Brandon, who stayed on to coach the Falcons when Meyer left for Utah in 2003. Meanwhile, his defensive coordinator at Bowling Green, Tim Beckman, went on to become the head coach at Toledo in 2009 before taking over at Illinois in 2012.

"It was another blessing to be with Urban," Beckman said prior to his Fighting Illini facing the Buckeyes in 2014. "He helped me with an opportunity of making myself better as a defensive coordinator. And there's a lot of things we still do in this program, and what I did at Toledo that have a little Urban Meyer flavor."

After arriving in Salt Lake City, Meyer's coaching tree only expanded.

In 2004, he hired a defensive line coach named Gary Andersen, who went on to become the head coach at Utah State, Wisconsin, and Oregon State. In 2014, Meyer's Buckeyes battled Andersen's Badgers in the 2014 Big Ten Championship Game, a 59–0 Ohio State victory, which would prove to be Andersen's final game at Wisconsin before leaving for Oregon State.

Although he only served as Andersen's boss for a single season with the Utes, it's clear Meyer left a lasting impression on his future Big Ten foe. Unsurprisingly, his sentiments are similar to that of Meyer's former assistants.

"Coach Meyer let us do what we wanted to do," Andersen said a day prior to the 2014 Big Ten title game. "We were very successful, had a great year. I learned a lot, a lot from Coach Meyer in that year in a lot of different ways. I put that into a lot of my philosophies as a head football coach."

As Meyer moved on to Florida in 2005, his success at Utah—much like at Bowling Green—led to the Utes making an in-house hire. After serving as Utah's defensive coordinator for the previous decade with his final two years of polishing coming under Meyer, Kyle Whittingham was promoted to head coach in 2005.

Whittingham has remained in the position ever since, amassing an impressive 103–50 record, including three 10-win seasons and an additional 13–0 campaign in 2008.

"I learned a ton, but probably organization skills and the way to run a program on a day-to-day basis," Whittingham told Fox Sports' Bruce Feldman when asked what he learned most from Meyer. "We could tell you what we're going to be doing any day of the year, a year out. We've got everything mapped out and there's nothing left to chance. It's not a seat-of-your-pants deal. Everything has a reason for what you do. He's very methodical in his approach."

It was in Gainesville, however, where Meyer's coaching tree truly blossomed.

During his six seasons with the Gators, Meyer oversaw the development of five different future head coaches—with perhaps more still to come.

It started with Mullen, who followed Meyer to Florida after having served as his grad assistant at Notre Dame, quarterbacks coach at Bowling Green and Utah and offensive coordinator with the Gators. After two national championships sandwiched Tim Tebow's Heisman Trophy–winning season of 2007, Mississippi State opted to hire Mullen at the end of the 2008 campaign.

In eight seasons in Starkville, Mullen's Bulldogs have compiled a 60–42 record and produced now–Dallas Cowboys star quarterback Dak Prescott.

Of all the future head coaches Meyer has helped produce, one would think Mullen would be the one he left the biggest imprint on. And while there are many similarities in the way the two have gone about running their respective programs, Mullen is also quick to note that there's no way to truly replicate Meyer's approach.

"One of the things you'll see, a lot of guys on the tree, the outline doesn't change. How everybody applies that outline is probably very different. I've had people say, 'You run your program very similar to how Urban runs his,' but if you're there watching it, it's very different," Mullen said during an appearance at Ohio State's coaching clinic in 2015. "You can't try to imitate him or be like him. You have to be like yourself. Use this outline and apply it to your beliefs as a program, and you're going to be successful. Guys that were assistants understood that. I think that's what he always encouraged people to do: coach to your strengths. This is the outline that works, and apply your strengths to that outline."

After Mullen moved, the Florida staff essentially became a pipeline for fellow programs.

In 2009, Louisville hired Gators defensive coordinator Charlie Strong, who compiled an impressive 37–15 record in four seasons with the Cardinals. In 2014, Texas hired Strong as its head coach, but his time in Austin didn't prove as fruitful. After failing to post a winning record in three seasons with the Longhorns, Strong was fired and replaced by another member of the Meyer coaching tree in Herman.

Strong, however, wouldn't stay unemployed for long. At the end of the 2016 season, Southern Florida hired him as its head coach.

Meyer lost another offensive coordinator at the end of the 2010 season when Steve Addazio took over as the head coach at Temple, where he spent two seasons before being hired by Boston College. In six seasons as a head coach, Addazio has recorded a 36–38 record.

That same off-season, North Texas hired Gators defensive line coach and former Iowa State head coach Dan McCarney. He was fired midway through the 2015 campaign after posting a 22–32 record in 4½ seasons.

And although his time in Gainesville didn't directly lead to a head coaching gig, former Florida safeties coach Doc Holliday became the head coach at Marshall in 2010. With a 53–37 record to his credit, the 2014 Conference USA Coach of the Year has proven to be one of Meyer's most successful ex-assistants.

While Meyer has cited the attrition his staff endured as one of the reasons his time at Florida was cut short, he's managed to successfully deal with similar departures at Ohio State. In his first five seasons in Columbus, four assistants have moved on to become head coaches, with another two taking assistant jobs in the NFL.

The first to leave was co–defensive coordinator Everett Withers, who accepted the head coaching position at James Madison in 2014 and has since moved on to the same role at Texas State. And although Meyer's time with the former NFL assistant was brief, his imprint remains on Withers' programs.

That was apparent during Withers' introductory press conference at JMU, when he referenced "competitive spirit" and going "from point A to point B in 4 to 6 seconds with relentless effort"—both staples of the Meyer lexicon. It's no coincidence either that an Ohio State helmet and jersey were each put on prominent display in his office at the Virginia-based FCS program.

Perhaps the most important part of Withers' brief time in Columbus, however, was the succession chain his departure led to on the Buckeyes' staff.

In need of a co–defensive coordinator capable of fixing Ohio State's passing defense, Meyer sought out one of the best in the business in Arkansas defensive coordinator Chris Ash. For Ash, the attraction was mutual. In hopes of becoming a head coach sooner rather than later, the longtime Bret Bielema assistant jumped at the opportunity to learn under one of college football's best.

"Chris came to Ohio State for that very reason," Meyer said. "He wanted to compete for a championship and wanted to be a head coach."

In two years, he accomplished both. It took just one season for Ash to help transform the Buckeyes defense into a national championship–winning unit and at the end of the 2015 campaign, he accepted the head coaching job at Rutgers.

Meyer's coaching tree is extensive. In addition to producing Gary Andersen, currently at Oregon State, Meyer has also influenced Tom Herman (Texas), Charlie Strong (South Florida), Kyle Whittingham (Utah), and many more.

Just like so many others before him, Ash has attempted to mirror his new program after his old one. That's why as the Scarlet Knights took the field for their first spring practice under their new head coach, the helmets of their first-year players were adorned with black stripes—another Meyer staple.

As for his own program, Meyer remained as aggressive when it came to replacing Ash as he was when he first hired him. In a move that came as a shock to many in the football world, Ohio State hired former Rutgers and Tampa Bay Buccaneers head coach Greg Schiano as its new co–defensive coordinator following Ash's departure. Although he appeared completely overqualified for a coordinating gig, Schiano noted if there was ever a head coach he'd be willing to work for, it'd be Meyer.

"I have kind of gone back for a master's degree in coaching under someone I'm very close with," Schiano told the Associated Press in 2016.

Considering Schiano has drawn interest from Southern California, Miami (Florida), and Oregon since being fired from the Buccaneers at the end of 2013, Meyer's ability to keep him in Columbus as an assistant for two years may speak to Meyer's star power as a head coach more than anything else.

Schiano's presence in Columbus is also especially important considering that at the end of the 2016 season, Meyer lost his third defensive coordinator in four years when Luke Fickell accepted the head coaching job at Cincinnati.

An Ohio State lifer save for a two-year stint as an assistant at Akron in 2000s, Fickell's stint as the Buckeyes' interim coach in 2011 left him with a sour taste in his mouth when it came to running his own program. It wasn't until he had spent a full five seasons under Meyer that he made a conscious effort to seek out head coaching vacancies. And when he did, it was telling he was able to land a job as highly sought after as the Bearcats—thanks in no small part to a half a decade under Meyer's tutelage.

"[Meyer] pushed me to the point of where I am today to be a head football coach," Fickell said in his introductory press conference.

Meyer's career has also helped produce rising assistants such as Mike Sanford, Mike Vrabel, and Stan Drayton, each of whom could eventually find himself running his own program or NFL team. As long as Meyer's success continues, his coaching tree won't stop growing anytime soon.

No branch, however, may grow as quickly as Herman's did. Two years after being mentored by Meyer, the former Houston head coach is now his rival on the recruiting trail. It's a long way from where Herman stood in 2011, convinced he was on the wrong end of a prank call when Meyer first inquired about the then–Iowa State offensive coordinator's services.

Like many before him, Herman spoke to all he learned under Meyer in his three seasons at Ohio State.

"People ask me all the time, what was the thing I took away the most? There was a thousand things I took away from Coach Meyer, but I think probably the biggest one is the practice of alignment," Herman said.

"From your assistant coaches to your strength staff to your support staff to your training room to the academic people to the expectations, it can't be okay to show up two minutes late for a tutor but not be okay to show up two minutes late for a position meeting. So you have to be aligned in everything that you do or else kids oftentimes have a way of going off the reservation a little bit."

If Meyer really did run his own coaching school, Herman would have graduated at the top of his class.

As it currently stands, Meyer has more former assistants currently running FBS programs than either Nick Saban or Jim Harbaugh. And his 11 assistants have combined for a .559 winning percentage. For comparison's sake, Harbaugh's four former assistants now running their own programs possess a .575 record, while Saban's six ex-assistants lay claim to a .683 winning rate.

But when factoring both the quality and quantity of Meyer has helped produce, there may not be a healthier coaching tree in all of college football.

★ ★ ★

Recruiting, Recruiting, Recruiting

During a Q&A session with ESPN analyst Kirk Herbstreit on the 2013 Buckeyes Cruise for Cancer following his first season as Ohio State's head coach, Urban Meyer was asked a question regarding his desire for his team to add more night games to its slate.

The Buckeyes had traditionally hosted just one such contest under the lights of Ohio Stadium—sometimes two. Meyer, however, made it clear he was open to adding more.

Much more.

"People are going to get tired of me saying that, because there's tradition about not having many in the Big Ten," Meyer said. "I love tradition, but I love recruiting better."

At the time, fans didn't make much of Meyer's comment and looked at it as little more than proof that unlike his predecessor, Jim Tressel, the Buckeyes' new head coach had a different way of dealing way of presenting his program to the press.

But as Meyer's tenure in Columbus carried on, the principle of loving tradition, but loving recruiting better might as well have served as a rallying cry for the Ohio State program under his watch.

"Recruiting is really important in the game of college football," he continued. "More important. Like, really important. More important than anything else. You get my point? The electric atmospheres we experienced at Penn State, I don't want to use the term 'SEC-ish,' but that was as good as there is."

Meyer has long referred to the recruiting trail as the lifeblood of his programs. And few coaches in the country have proved as capable of securing a steady stream of highly touted prospects to their team than Meyer has for the better part of the past two decades.

In an effort to stockpile his team with the nation's top talent, Meyer has relied on a multipronged approach. Like any successful coach, he's had help along the way. But what separates Meyer from the rest of his peers is his ability to take full advantage of his many resources.

What follows is a look at how Meyer has managed to consistently sign some of the nation's top classes over the course of his career.

Border Control

On National Signing Day 2017, Meyer signed what many considered to be a historic recruiting class. According to the 247Sports.com composite, which compiles the recruiting scores of its own along with those of other recruiting services, the Buckeyes' 21-man class possessed an average player score (94.47) higher than any other class in the website's history, dating back to 2000.

Yet as Meyer spoke to reporters at his signing-day press conference, an elephant in the room loomed large. Despite the quality of player in Ohio State's haul, the class possessed relatively little Ohio flavor, with just seven of the 21 signees hailing from the Buckeye State.

Even Meyer and Buckeyes director of player personnel Mark Pantoni conceded that wasn't enough.

"No, it's not. No, 50 percent is kind of the mark that I've been trying to [hit]," Meyer said. "I keep it right in front of me and I stare at it and make sure that we're doing right."

This, however, served as the exception in Meyer's recruiting track record. And even dating back to his days at Florida, where competition for the state's top players is fierce, Meyer routinely secured the services of the top players in the Sunshine State.

"At Florida when you walked into a home it was either a 'Nole, 'Cane, or a Gator," Meyer recalled in 2014. "And you usually look on the wall and figure out where you're at."

Yet even when Meyer entered a house that had been predisposed to favoring Florida State or Miami, the then–Gators head coach had a habit of flipping their allegiances to Florida.

After only signing four of the state's top 25 players in 2005, Meyer signed 10 of Florida's top 25 players in his second Gators class, which marked his first full recruiting cycle while in charge in Gainesville. In 2007, he kicked his Sunshine State efforts up a notch, inking seven of the state's top 10 players and in 2010, he would sign six of the state's top 10 and nine of its top 25 prospects.

In both quality and quantity, Meyer's classes with the Gators were full of Florida flavor.

That trend would continue upon Meyer's arrival at Ohio State, although he admitted routinely recruiting the Buckeyes' backyard wasn't as easy as it had been in Gainesville. Most notably, Ohio high school football lacks a spring football period, which can lead to some players in the Buckeye State developing later than other prospects across the nation.

Nevertheless, 15 of the 25 signees in Meyer's first Ohio State class hailed from his new home state and in 2013, 11 of the Buckeyes' 2013 signees were Ohio prospects. Meyer may not always hit the 50-50 split that he strives for between recruiting his home base and the national landscape, but both he and his staff have made their preference for Ohio-based prospects clear.

"Trust me, we uncover every stone and rock for kids in the state of Ohio," said Pantoni, who runs the Buckeyes' recruiting operation.

Meyer's office at the Woody Hayes Athletic Center is no doubt a valuable tool when he hosts recruits.

"We spend unlimited resources on them. We want to sign as many kids from Ohio as we can, and that's our ultimate goal.

"Ohio's our first [priority] and then we'll branch out to the Midwest."

Those efforts have resulted in in-state success reminiscent of Meyer's six-year stint with the Gators. In 2012, he signed the state's top-ranked player, Adolphus Washington, and half of Ohio's top 10. In 2014, he signed Ohio's five highest-ranked players and in 2015, it was six of the top 10. In all but one of Meyer's first six recruiting cycles at Ohio State, the top-ranked player in the state of Ohio has become a Buckeye.

That isn't a coincidence.

"If we have to, we'll go to the Southeast or Texas," Pantoni admitted. "But our ultimate goal is to get Ohio kids who understand the tradition, the rivalry, and who grew up as Buckeyes. So that's important to us."

But as Pantoni said—and the numbers show—Meyer hasn't been afraid to venture outside state borders either.

Going National

While an ideal Ohio State class for Meyer might consist of half Ohio prospects, half national prospects, circumstances sometime dictate a different direction. Through his first six recruiting cycles, Meyer has missed his goal of a 50-50 split, with 73 of his first 152 signees (46.2 percent) having hailed from the Buckeye State.

In this sense, Ohio State's philosophy is a little simpler. Recruiting kids from Ohio might be the preference. But it's far from the end all, be all.

"We want to really recruit the state of Ohio because we love Ohio, we love the coaches here, we love the players here," said Buckeyes wide receivers coach Zach Smith, who doubles as the team's recruiting coordinator. "But at the end of the day, we need the best quarterback in the country, the best receiver in the country. So we're gonna get them wherever they are."

As Pantoni referenced, when the Buckeyes have strayed outside of Ohio, it often hasn't been too far outside the Midwest. Ohio State has maintained a strong presence in Pennsylvania and across the Eastern Seaboard, where Meyer built inroads throughout his time at Florida.

Speaking of Florida, the Buckeyes have also maintained success in the Sunshine State, particularly at prep powerhouse St. Thomas Aquinas, which has given Ohio State Joey and Nick Bosa, as well as 2017 four-star wide receiver Trevon Grimes.

Under Meyer, however, the Buckeyes have also ventured into what had previously been foreign territory as far as their recruiting efforts were concerned. In Jim Tressel's 11 recruiting cycles at Ohio State, the Buckeyes had signed just three prospects from the talent-rich state of Texas.

Meyer matched those efforts in his 2013 class alone, signing one of the nation's top linebackers, Mike Mitchell, a premier athlete in Dontre Wilson, and his quarterback of the future in J.T. Barrett.

The presence of former Buckeyes offensive coordinator Tom Herman helped the Buckeyes forge their formerly untapped pipeline, but so too did the national appeal of Meyer.

"It's not challenging when you go 12–0 and Urban Meyer's your head coach and you're wearing the block O on your shirt," said Herman, who headed up Ohio State's recruiting efforts in the Lone Star State from 2012 to '14, in 2013. "Those three things certainly help you."

Four years later, the Buckeyes would only increase their efforts in Texas, signing three of the state's top six players. In addition to Texas, Ohio State has also made recruiting inroads into California, Nevada, and Georgia with Meyer at its helm.

For the Buckeyes, Ohio might remain the priority. But Meyer also isn't going to hesitate to go wherever he needs to in order to assemble the most-talented roster possible.

"Ohio State is a national brand and will always be and always has been," Meyer said. "The success we've had recently and the exposure that this program has had for the right reasons has really been beneficial."

Hidden Gems

Not all of Meyer's recruiting efforts, however, have been all about chasing stars—in-state and out. While Meyer is known as a premier recruiter, some of his best players have come as a result of identifying talent on his own.

Such was the case in his first summer in Columbus, when an undersized linebacker from nearby New Albany High School repeatedly attended the Buckeyes' summer camps. And although Meyer wasn't quick to extend a scholarship offer to Darron Lee, the future Ohio State star remained undeterred.

"He came to camp, like five or six times," Meyer recalled. "I rejected him probably four times," Meyer said. "Shows you how good an evaluator I am. The thing that we loved about him, he kept competing."

Eventually, Meyer relented, extending a scholarship to the little known three-star prospect, which Lee accepted on the spot. And although the Ohio State head coach often credits former Buckeyes defensive coordinator and linebackers coach Luke Fickell with finding Lee, there's not a scholarship offer the Buckeyes send out that their head coach hasn't signed off on.

"Someone posted a picture of a skinny-neck quarterback from New Albany," Meyer said referring to a tweet posted by Pantoni depicting Lee's transformation prior to the New York Jets selecting him in the first round of the 2016 NFL draft. "Now [he's] going to the NFL."

Meyer's tenure in Columbus has been littered with such success stories for hidden gems on the recruiting trail. In addition to Lee, formerly lightly recruited players like Cardale Jones, Tyvis Powell, and Michael Thomas each played a key role in the Buckeyes' run to a national championship in 2014.

Two years later, Ohio State clinched its second appearance in the College Football Playoff, with a roster that possessed two unanimous All-Americans. Center Pat Elflein was the lowest-rated recruit in the Buckeyes' 2012 class, while safety Malik Hooker was a three-star prospect who only had one full season playing football under his belt when he committed to Ohio State in the summer of 2013. Additionally, defensive tackle Robert Landers, a former three-star prospect, played a key role as a rotational defensive lineman throughout the Buckeyes' run to their playoff appearance.

As is the case with most things recruiting, there's a balance that needs to be struck. The more spots in a class you fill with premier five- and four-star prospects, the less room that exists for potential projects like Lee and Hooker. In Ohio State's 2017 class, it's hard to find a true developmental player-type. The lone three-star prospects in the class are kicker Blake Haubeil and wide receiver Ellijah Gardiner, who was a late addition when a previously committed five-star opted to take his talents elsewhere.

Meyer's penchant for finding talent, regardless of a player's recruiting ranking, dates back to his time at Utah. In his first class in Salt Lake City, Meyer signed a two-star safety named Eric Weddle, who would go on to make four Pro Bowls throughout a still-ongoing NFL career.

Of course, recruiting is only half the battle. It's what a prospect does in his actual college career that truly counts.

But just like on the recruiting trail, when it comes to Ohio State's player development, Meyer's programs have been tough to top.

Players in the Pros

Having produced a total of 61 NFL draft picks, including 16 first-round selections over the course of his career, Meyer has proved to be one of the most adept college coaches in the country when it comes to putting players in the pros. Among active coaches, Meyer entered the 2017 NFL draft having totaled the fourth most total draft picks and second most first-rounders.

What follows is a look at the players Meyer has been responsible for helping develop into pro prospects throughout his coaching career and the success they have gone on to enjoy at the next level.

Bowling Green

Technically, Meyer never had a player drafted under his watch in either of his two seasons at Bowling Green, although he does deserve credit for the development of quarterback Josh Harris. A converted running back, Harris starred as Meyer's starting signal-caller for the better part of his two seasons with the Falcons before totaling 4,643 total yards and 40 touchdowns in his senior season in 2003.

The Baltimore Ravens selected Harris in the sixth round of the 2004 NFL draft. He would go on to spend two seasons on the roster of the Cleveland Browns before stints in the Canadian Football League, Arena League, and Continental Indoor Football League.

Center Scott Mruczkowski, a member of Meyer's first recruiting class at Bowling Green, was selected in the seventh round of the 2005 NFL draft and spent seven seasons with the San Diego Chargers.

Utah

After failing to have a prospect selected in the entire 2004 NFL draft, Meyer's final season in Salt Lake City would produce five players who would be picked in 2005.

At the top of the list was quarterback Alex Smith, whom the San Francisco 49ers selected with the draft's first overall pick. Smith spent seven seasons in San Francisco, compiling a 19–5–1 record as a starter in his final two years with the franchise before losing his starting job to Colin Kaepernick. In 2013, the 49ers traded Smith to the Kansas City Chiefs, where he's won 11 games in three of his first four seasons. Over the course of his first 11 seasons, Smith has compiled a 79–56–1 record as a starter, 27,846 passing yards, 157 passing touchdowns, and 91 interceptions.

The New York Jets selected defensive tackle Sione Po'uha in the third round of the 2005 draft and the former All–Mountain West selection went on to spend eight seasons with the franchise, tallying 263 career tackles and 4.5 sacks. In the draft's sixth round, the Pittsburgh Steelers selected offensive guard Chris Kemoeatu, who served as a starter on the Steelers team that would go on to win Super Bowl XLIII. Kemoeatu's career with Pittsburgh ultimately lasted seven seasons.

Rounding out the selections out of Utah in 2005 were wideout Paris Warren and defensive end Jonathan Fanene, each of whom was picked in the draft's seventh round. Warren would go on to spend four seasons with the Tampa Bay Buccaneers, catching five balls for 63 yards. Fanene, meanwhile, enjoyed a seven-year career with the Cincinnati Bengals, tallying 66 tackles, 13.5 sacks, and an interception.

Florida

2006

Meyer's first year in Gainesville would get off to a slow start as far as producing pros. Three players from the 2005 Gators were picked in the 2006 NFL draft, including second-round pick Chad Jackson, sixth-rounder Jeremy Mincey, and seventh-round selection Dee Webb.

Jackson spent two seasons with the New England Patriots and two with the Denver Broncos, primarily serving as a return specialist. Mincey enjoyed a 10-year career with the 49ers, Jacksonville Jaguars, Broncos, and Dallas Cowboys, tallying 215 tackles and 26 sacks. Webb spent two seasons with the Jaguars before embarking on a career in the CFL.

It wouldn't take long for Meyer to add to his NFL draft résumé.

2007

Following Meyer's first national championship with the Gators in 2006, nine players from the Florida roster were selected in the 2007 NFL draft.

Among that group was a duo of first-round picks in the draft's No. 17 pick, defensive end Jarvis Moss, and No. 21 selection, Reggie Nelson. Moss would spend five combined seasons with the Broncos and Oakland Raiders, recording 48 tackles and six career sacks. Nelson would emerge as one of the NFL's top players at his position and is still in the midst of a more-than-decadelong career, having earned two Pro Bowl selections over the course of his time with the Jaguars, Bengals, and Raiders.

In addition to Moss, three more players from the Gators' dominant defensive line would be selected in the 2007 draft, with end Ray McDonald going in the third round and tackles Marcus Thomas and Joe Cohen each being picked in the fourth round. McDonald spent eight seasons with the 49ers from 2007 to '14, posting 19.5 career sacks. Thomas, meanwhile, spent five seasons with the Broncos and Cohen saw only sporadic playing time in stints with the 49ers, Miami Dolphins, Raiders, and Detroit Lions that combined to last just three years.

The Tennessee Titans selected cornerback Ryan Smith in the sixth round of the 2007 draft, but the All-SEC selection would fail to make it past training camp with the Titans. Wide receiver Dallas Baker, running back DeShawn Wynn, and linebacker Brandon Siler were each picked in the draft's seventh round, with each finding varying success despite his late selection.

Baker spent three seasons with the Steelers, but only caught one pass before embarking on a career in the CFL. Wynn would spend three seasons on the roster of the Green Bay Packers before splitting the 2010 season between the New Orleans Saints and 49ers, tallying 332 career rushing yards and five touchdowns. Siler, the draft's No. 240 overall selection, spent four seasons with the San Diego Chargers and two more with the Chiefs and recorded 180 career tackles.

2008

A young 2007 Gators team would lead to Meyer's smallest draft class at Florida the following spring, although defensive end Derrick Harvey would become Meyer's highest-picked player since Alex Smith when the Jaguars selected him with the 2008 draft's No. 8 overall pick. Harvey's pro career, however, would last just three seasons in Jacksonville with an additional year in Denver as the BCS National Championship Game MVP totaled 92 tackles and eight career sacks.

In the third round, the Bengals selected wide receiver Andre Caldwell, who would become the only other ex-Gator player picked in the 2008 draft. Caldwell went on to enjoy an eight-year NFL career, split between four seasons with the Bengals and four with the Broncos, tallying 156 career receptions for 1,509 yards and 11 scores.

2009

Despite winning the 2008 BCS national championship, the Gators would produce another relatively small draft class in 2009, one that consisted solely of pass-catchers.

The Minnesota Vikings selected Percy Harvin in the first round with the No. 22 pick, and the former Florida star would go on to record 353 career receptions for 4,026 yards and 22 touchdowns, in addition to 927 rushing yards and five touchdowns, over the course of an eight-year career with the Vikings, Seattle Seahawks, New York Jets, and Buffalo Bills. Harvin also served as one of football's top kick returners in his time in the pros, recording 4,127 career kick-return yards.

The Raiders picked wide receiver Louis Murphy in the fourth round of the 2009 draft and the former Gators wideout has since enjoyed an eight-year career split among the Raiders, Carolina Panthers, New York Giants, and Tampa Bay Buccaneers. Over the course of his career, Murphy has recorded 161 receptions for 2,293 yards and 10 touchdowns.

In the fifth round, the Philadelphia Eagles picked tight end Cornelius Ingram, whose pro career never got off the ground due to injuries spent during time on the rosters of the Eagles, Detroit Lions, and Broncos.

The small draft classes produced by Florida in 2008 and 2009 would prove to be aberrations in Meyer's time in Gainesville.

2010

Coming off a 26–2 run in the previous two seasons, Florida's 2010 draft class produced nine picks, matching Meyer's previous high with the Gators.

The group would include a new high for Meyer with three first-round selections, including a pair of repeat Pro Bowlers in cornerback Joe Haden, whom the Cleveland Browns picked with the draft's No. 7 overall pick, and center Maurkice Pouncey, whom the Steelers selected No. 18 overall.

With the draft's No. 25 pick, the Broncos made Tim Tebow Meyer's second quarterback to be picked in the first round. A highly polarizing pro prospect, Tebow spent two seasons in Denver, leading the Broncos to a playoff victory in 2011, before joining the Jets for a single season and then failing to make the regular season rosters of either the Patriots or Eagles. As of 2017, Tebow was attempting to catch on as a baseball player in the New York Mets minor league system.

Three more ex-Gators would be picked in the 2010 draft's second round, including linebacker Jermaine Cunningham, defensive end Carlos Dunlap, and linebacker Brandon Spikes. Over the course of five seasons with the Patriots, 49ers, and Jets, Cunningham tallied 60 tackles and 3.5 sacks, while Dunlap has been one of Meyer's best pro players, having made two Pro Bowls and recording 57 sacks in his first seven seasons with the Bengals. After four seasons with the Patriots, Spikes joined the Bills and has been responsible for 349 tackles and two sacks in his six-year career.

The Chicago Bears selected safety Major Wright in the 2010 draft's third round and he has since enjoyed a seven-year career, having totaled nine career interceptions between his time with the Bears and Buccaneers. In the fourth round, the Patriots picked tight end Aaron Hernandez, who recorded 175 receptions, 1,956 yards, and 18 touchdowns in his three-year career. The final ex-Gator to come off the board in the 2010 draft was fifth-round pick Riley Cooper, who spent six seasons with the Eagles, recording 169 catches for 2,418 yards and 18 touchdowns.

2011

In Meyer's final draft class in Gainesville, the Gators added four prospects to his collection of pro players.

The Dolphins picked center Mike Pouncey with the No. 15 pick of the 2011 draft's first round and he has since enjoyed three Pro Bowl selections throughout his six-year career. In the second round, the Steelers selected offensive tackle Marcus Gilbert, who has similarly been a mainstay on the franchise's offensive line for the past six seasons.

The Buccaneers added Ahmad Black in the draft's fifth round, although the former Florida safety's pro career only lasted three seasons.

In the seventh round, the Washington Redskins made Maurice Haurt the third ex-Gator offensive lineman to be picked in the 2011 draft. Hurt would spend three seasons with the franchise.

Other players who played for Meyer at Florida before being picked in later drafts include but aren't limited to running back Chris Rainey, linebacker Jelani Jenkins, tight end Jordan Reed, safety Matt Elam, and defensive tackle Sharrif Floyd.

Ohio State
2013

After arriving at Ohio State in 2012, Meyer inherited a roster lacking in ready-made pro talent, but did manage to produce three picks in the 2013 NFL draft.

The New York Giants selected defensive tackle Jonathan Hankins in the second round of the 2013 draft and the former All-American has since enjoyed a promising pro career in the Big Apple. In four seasons with the Giants, Hankins has recorded 140 tackles and 10 sacks, earning second-team All-NFL honors in 2014.

Two rounds later, the Baltimore Ravens selected reigning Big Ten Defensive Player of the Year John Simon. After spending his rookie season with the Ravens, Simon was signed off the team's practice squad by the Houston Texans, whom he has since become a consistent starter for.

One of Meyer's more impressive jobs when it comes to developing a pro prospect came in the 2013 draft's seventh round. After spending the first three seasons of his college career as a tight end, Reid Fragel converted to offensive tackle in his senior season under Meyer and showed enough in just one year to warrant the Bengals using a seventh-round pick to select the former project. Fragel has since spent time on the practice and off-season squads of the Browns, Falcons, Chiefs, and Vikings, in addition to playing a part of the 2015 season with the Buccaneers.

2014

Like at Florida, Meyer's second season in Columbus saw him strengthen his program's pipeline to the NFL. Six ex-Buckeyes were selected in the 2014 NFL draft, including a pair of first-round defenders in linebacker Ryan Shazier and cornerback Bradley Roby.

Shazier has become one of the centerpieces of the Steelers defense and Roby played an integral part in the Broncos' Super Bowl championship season in 2015. Two more Ohio State players were picked in the draft's second round, with offensive lineman Jack Mewhort and running back Carlos Hyde having solidified themselves as starters on the Indianapolis Colts and 49ers, respectively.

Another solid pro from Ohio State came off the board in the draft's fifth round, when the Green Bay Packers selected center Corey Linsley. Linsley has served as the Packers' starting center since his rookie season, earning PFWA All-Rookie honors in 2014.

The St. Louis Rams picked former Buckeyes captain Christian Bryant in the draft's seventh round. He has since seen time on the practice squad of the Giants and on the active roster of the Arizona Cardinals.

2015

Five players from Ohio State would be picked in the 2015 NFL draft following the Buckeyes' run to the first-ever College Football Playoff championship. The Jets selected wideout Devin Smith in the second round with the

No. 37 overall pick, the Broncos picked tight end Jeff Heuerman in the third round, the Steelers selected cornerback Doran Grant in the fourth round, and the Jaguars added defensive tackle Michael Bennett in the sixth round, the same round in which the Redskins picked wideout Evan Spencer.

Thus far, the production of Meyer's third Ohio State class has been limited, although Smith has shown flashes as a deep threat in New York.

You wouldn't be able to say the same about the Buckeyes' following class.

2016

Not only did Ohio State set the record for most players picked in the first four rounds of the modern draft era with 12—but the Buckeyes rookies delivered in 2016 as well.

No. 4 overall pick and running back Ezekiel Elliott was a break-out star on the Dallas Cowboys, totaling 1,631 rushing yards and 15 touchdowns in his rookie campaign, while the player picked before him, defensive end Joey Bosa, won Rookie of the Year honors with a 10.5-sack season for the San Diego Chargers.

Fellow first-rounders Eli Apple, Taylor Decker, and Darron Lee enjoyed significant playing time as rookies for their respective teams, while second-round pick Michael Thomas caught 92 passes for 1,137 yards and nine touchdowns for the New Orleans Saints, who also feature second-round selection and former Buckeyes safety Vonn Bell.

Third-round picks Adolphus Washington, Braxton Miller, and Nick Vannett each managed to get on the field as rookies, as did fourth-rounders Joshua Perry and Cardale Jones.

Not only did Ohio State deliver on draft day, but by the end of the 2016 NFL season, ESPN proclaimed the Buckeyes' draft class "the best rookie class ever."

2017

In 2017, Ohio State added to its haul. When the New Orleans Saints selected cornerback Marshon Lattimore with the No. 11 pick in the draft, he became the first of three Buckeyes defensive backs to be picked in the first round, making Ohio State the first program to accomplish that feat since Miami (Florida) in 2002. In addition to Lattimore, safety Malik Hooker (No. 15 overall to the Indianapolis Colts) and cornerback Gareon Conley (No. 24 to the Oakland Raiders), and former Buckeyes Curtis Samuel (Carolina Panthers), Raekwon McMillan (Miami Dolphins), Pat Elflein (Minnesota Vikings) and Noah Brown (Dallas Cowboys) heard their names called by the end of the 2017 draft.

How each Buckeyes draftee will fare in his respective NFL career remains to be seen. But as his track record shows, putting productive players into the pros has been a theme throughout Meyer's coaching career.

★ ★ ★

The Godfather of the Spread

Urban Meyer's arrival in Columbus presented Ohio State with an interesting dichotomy when it came to the direction of the Buckeyes offense.

On the one hand, Meyer had grown up idolizing old-school coaches like Woody Hayes and studying under the tutelage of Earle Bruce. On the other, Meyer was not only a proponent of the spread offense—he was one of its innovators.

"We're going to run the spread. The spread is also going to have some I-formation pro style in it which we've always done, we'll try to adapt it the best we can," Meyer said at his introductory press conference. "If you look at our plays, it's the same plays that I was brought up on, split zone and off-tackle power. That's a staple here at Ohio State.

"The one thing that our offense that we always tried to take great pride in is Big Ten I-formation power football. We just do it from a unique formation, sometimes do it with a 240-pound quarterback."

But while Meyer has been steadfast in asserting that his offense possesses the same power elements that served as staples of his OSU predecessors' offensive philosophies, he remains an innovator when it comes college football's modern offenses. For the better part of the past two decades, the spread offense has become not just an equalizer for undermanned programs, but a necessity for teams looking to exploit matchups while making the most of its talent.

Looking across the landscape of college football, it's tough to find a program that hasn't implemented at least some spread elements into its offense, including Alabama, which had previously relied on more Hayes-like power running schemes. The prominence of the spread in today's game was most apparent in the inaugural College Football Playoff, in which two spread programs—Ohio State and Oregon—squared off with the national title on the line.

But before the spread offense rose to the forefront of the college football world, it was merely the brainchild of an assistant coach in South Bend, Indiana, who was daydreaming about his first head coaching gig.

Spread Origins

By the time Meyer's time as an assistant coach had neared its end, a traditional offense was practically all he knew. After being groomed under the likes of Bruce, Sonny Lubick, Lou Holtz, and Bob Davie, the then–wide receivers and special teams coach had become accustomed to I-formations and one-back sets.

But following a 1998 season in which Notre Dame ranked No. 42 in total offense, Meyer could sense a change coming in the college football landscape. Defenses hadn't just caught up; they were continuing to evolve. And as a result, offenses were going to have to find a way to keep pace.

"The complexities and talent on defense just made it harder and harder to move the ball," Meyer recalled in 2012.

So Meyer and his then–graduate assistant with the Fighting Irish, Dan Mullen, packed their bags and headed for Louisville, where former Washington offensive coordinator Scott Linehan had just joined John L. Smith's Louisville staff. Meyer had only anticipated staying for a day, maybe two, but found himself enthralled by Linehan's ability to diagram plays out of nontraditional sets.

"We had to go buy toothbrushes because I was so enamored with the style of play," Meyer said.

Linehan's philosophy was relatively simple; the more players you have packaged together in close proximity, the easier it becomes for a defense to not only defend them, but apply pressures. Mix in Linehan's less-than-conservative approach and it's easy to see why his offensive philosophy had such profound impact on Meyer.

"Spread the field, be extremely, extremely aggressive," Meyer said of Linehan's line of thinking. "And the biggest issue is how to handle pressures. The tighter the formation, the more pressures. I mean, it's really numbers. If you're in here, you've got to worry about 11 guys. If you're out here, you've got to worry about six. Because they have to cover all those guys. So it's just a different philosophy.

"I started thinking, 'What would I do offensively if I became a head coach?'"

Two years later, Meyer would find out.

Sitting in a team meeting room in Bowling Green, Ohio, Meyer and his assistants plotted what would become the model for the modern spread offense.

"We all sat in that old nasty meeting room in Bowling Green, Ohio, where every time it rained, the water would drip down on the table," Meyer recalled of an offensive staff that included himself; offensive coordinator Gregg Brandon; offensive line coach Greg Strudrawa; and Mullen, now the Falcons quarterbacks coach. "We sat there for the month of February and the month of March—every morning coming in for 10 hours—from the huddle to the snap count, because there was no other model. Northwestern was doing some of it at the time and Rich Rodriguez was doing some at the time. So we kind of watched them a little bit as well. But we developed our own."

It wouldn't take long for Bowling Green to put it to the test.

Facing a more talented Missouri team in his head coaching debut, Meyer had no choice but to put his new offensive system to the test. And as the Falcons spread their undermanned offensive roster across the field, the Tigers had no choice but to try to cover them as conventionally as they could.

"We got on a plane and had some receivers that couldn't catch," Meyer recalled. "So we did empty and we put the guys over here but no one knew that. So Missouri still covered them."

The result was a 20–13 Bowling Green victory and the birth of a new offensive era in college football.

"We were the novelty," Meyer recalls. "Fifty-two scholarship players, and we won that game. It was because they had a hard time getting lined up."

Pivot

Over the course of his career, Meyer hasn't just invented a new style of offense, but a new position as well.

Referred to as the "pivot" or 'H-back' position in Meyer's version of the spread, his offenses at Bowling Green, Utah, Florida, and Ohio State have each featured running back–wide receiver hybrids equally capable of carrying the ball out of the backfield and catching it downfield.

But while the pivot has served as a staple of Meyer's teams at each of his four head coaching stops, its roots stem from his time as an assistant with the Fighting Irish.

After Notre Dame suffered an early-season loss to top-ranked Nebraska at the start of the 2000 season, Meyer found himself consoling an emotional David Givens in the postgame locker room. The Fighting Irish's best receiver and a future Super Bowl champion with the New England Patriots, Givens had been limited to just one reception for nine yards in Notre Dame's 27–24 overtime loss to the Cornhuskers and had grown frustrated by his impact—or lack thereof—on the game.

"He was really emotional," Meyer recalled in 2015. "I said, 'It's going to be okay, man. We'll bounce back.' He said, 'You don't understand, Coach. I didn't touch the ball.' He wasn't saying it like some kids, like, 'I need the damn ball,' not like that. Just, he didn't feel he helped the team win.

"I remember walking in the locker room, and I was very upset with myself that we did not get him the ball."

As a result, Meyer began diagramming different ways to feature his premier offensive weapons. Typically, those players would be receivers, who Meyer found had become too easy to neutralize—as was the case with Givens against Nebraska.

"It's hard to get receivers the ball," Meyer said. "If they roll up on you or double you, you can't get them the ball."

But Meyer found that if you lined a player up in the slot, it increased the number of ways he could contribute to a game plan. A receiver in the slot could run a traditional route, motion into the backfield and serve as a running back, or receive the ball on a direct handoff and become a ball carrier on a jet sweep.

The first player to play the position for Meyer was Bowling Green's Cole Magnum, who tallied 455 yards and four touchdowns on 26 receptions and 11 carries during the Falcons' 2002 campaign. At Utah, Meyer would inherit a pair of even-more-dynamic offensive weapons in wide receiver Paris Warren (933 yards, five touchdowns on 76 receptions and 20 carries in 2003) and tight end/running back Ben Moa (517 yards, nine touchdowns on 31 carries and 26 receptions in 2003).

Warren would go on to tally 1,233 total yards and 14 touchdowns during the Utes' undefeated 2004 campaign as the pivot appeared to have found a permanent place in Meyer's spread offense. It wasn't until he recruited the nation's top-ranked player in 2006, Percy Harvin, to play the position, however, that it truly rose to prominence as one of the country's premier positions.

After Harvin tallied nearly 4,000 total yards in three seasons in Gainesville before becoming a first-round pick in the 2009 NFL draft, Chris Rainey and Jeff Demps would attempt to fill his void at H-back in Meyer's final two seasons with the Gators.

At Ohio State, Meyer hardly inherited a player who possessed both the versatility and dynamic athleticism of Harvin and instead experimented with the likes of Jordan Hall and Corey "Philly" Brown to fill the void. Converted quarterback Braxton Miller would find some success at the spot in the 2015 campaign, but it wasn't until Curtis Samuel's emergence the following year that Meyer found the perfect player for his pivot position in Columbus.

Tallying 1,636 yards (865 receiving, 771 rushing) and 15 touchdowns, Samuel served as one of the nation's top playmakers in 2016, totaling more yards in a single season that Harvin ever did.

"If you're wondering what that position is, that's it," Meyer said of Samuel. "That's what the hybrid H does—he carries the ball in the backfield and he also catches the ball."

Spread Success

Obviously, it doesn't take a look at much more than Meyer's 165–29 career record to see that his spread offense has been a success. And over the course of his career, Meyer has coached some of the nation's top offenses, including a Utah unit that ranked third nationally in 2004, a trio of top-10 nationally ranked offenses at Florida, and a pair of top-five offenses at Ohio State in 2013 and 2014.

But more so than the exact numbers, Meyer's offensive units have been defined by defined by the players they've produced—particularly the quarterbacks. At Bowling Green, it was a running back–turned–NFL draft pick in Josh Harris. At Utah, it was the No. 1 pick of the 2005 NFL draft in Alex Smith. And at Florida, Tim Tebow transformed into one of the best players in the history of college football.

Meyer's crowning offensive achievement, however, came at Ohio State, where after Miller won back-to-back Big Ten MVP awards in 2012 and 2013, J.T. Barrett was named the conference's Quarterback of the Year in the same season that Cardale Jones led the Buckeyes to the College Football Playoff championship.

At that point, it seemed like any signal-caller was capable of finding success in Meyer's spread system—not that the Buckeyes head coach viewed that as a bad thing.

"I get a little upset when I hear, 'He's a system quarterback,'" Meyer said. "Damn right he is. He's not a grab-bag quarterback, I can promise you that. That's why I like the way we do our business."

Much like the rest of his offense, the results speak for themselves.

The All–Urban Meyer Team

If one were to compile an All–Urban Meyer team, it would double as collection of college football's top players from the past 15 years. Outside of Nick Saban, no other coach in the sport can lay claim to having coached as many premier players throughout his career as Meyer has.

Looking for a quarterback worthy of being selected first overall in the NFL draft? Meyer's coached one. A Heisman Trophy winner who changed the way we look at individual statistics in the modern era? Meyer's coached one of those as well.

Need multipurpose skill players, Cadillac-like running backs, and first-round-caliber offensive linemen? Check, check, and check.

And when it comes to the defensive side of the ball, there are almost too many pass-rush specialists, ball-hawking safeties, lockdown corners, and lightning-quick linebackers to count.

Even for a head coach who claims (in jest) to hate punters, Meyer's coached a few great ones of those too.

So what would an All-Meyer team look like, from his first year at Bowling Green to his most recent at Ohio State? No matter whom you pick at each position, there's likely to be plenty of debate. Nevertheless, here's my best attempt to put into perspective the ridiculous amount of talent Urban Meyer has coached in his 15 seasons as a head coach, based on the impact each made in his time under Meyer.

Quarterback: Tim Tebow (Florida)

When it comes to Meyer's history as a head coach, quarterback is probably the position possessing the highest number of qualified candidates to be considered his best. Amongst the group of signal-callers he's coached are a No. 1 overall NFL draft pick, a Heisman Trophy winner, and arguably the greatest quarterback in Ohio State history.

Of the quarterbacks to have run Meyer's spread offense, however, none has been as associated with him as Tim Tebow has.

A five-star prospect by way of Ponte Vedra Beach, Florida, Tebow arrived at Florida as one of the premier prospects in Meyer's highly touted 2006 recruiting class. And it didn't take long for the top-ranked signal-caller to make an impact in Gainesville.

Spelling senior starter Chris Leak in a two-quarterback system, Tebow provided Meyer with a dual-threat option behind center throughout the Gators' run to the 2006 BCS National Championship. Appearing in 14 games, the 6'3", 229-pound bruiser tallied 469 rushing yards and eight touchdowns on the ground, in addition to completing 22 of his 33 pass attempts for 358 yards and five touchdowns.

Between his two touchdown passes—including his infamous "jump pass"—in a top-10 win over LSU and his 39 rushing yards and touchdown in the BCS Championship Game against Ohio State, Florida likely doesn't win its first national title game if not for the presence of Tebow.

"He's a rock 'em, sock 'em kind of runner," LSU coach Les Miles said in 2006. "Florida used him to their advantage."

Tebow was just getting started.

In his first season as a full-time starter in 2007, Tebow revolutionized the way the nation looks at quarterback numbers. The first player in FBS history to both throw for 20 touchdowns and rush for 20 touchdowns in the same season, Tebow compiled 4,181 yards of total offense (3,286 passing, 895 rushing) and 55 total touchdowns (32 passing, 23 rushing) while helping lead the Gators to a 9–4 record. In the process, he became the first sophomore to win the Heisman Trophy.

A year later, Tebow would only add to his legacy, logging 3,419 yards of total offense and 42 total touchdowns while leading Florida to a 13–1 record and a second BCS National Championship in three seasons. In 2009, the Gators' bid for a repeat would fall short due to a loss in the SEC title game to Alabama, but Tebow put together another monster season with 3,805 total yards and 35 touchdowns.

By the time his college career came to an end, Tebow laid claim to five NCAA, 14 SEC, and 28 University of Florida records. He also ranks second all-time in college football history in passing efficiency with a career quarterback rating of 170.8.

A first-round pick of the Denver Broncos in 2010, Tebow's NFL career spanned three seasons, including a 2011 campaign that saw him help the Broncos to a playoff win over the Pittsburgh Steelers. He's currently in the midst of attempting to jump-start a pro baseball career in the New York Mets' minor league system.

But regardless of what's happened since his time in Gainesville came to an end, Tebow's college career remains one of the most storied in football history.

Second team: Alex Smith (Utah)
Honorable mention: J.T. Barrett (Ohio State), Braxton Miller (Ohio State), Josh Harris (Bowling Green)

Running Backs: Ezekiel Elliott (Ohio State), Carlos Hyde (Ohio State)

If Tim Tebow is the best player Urban Meyer has ever coached, then Ezekiel Elliott might be 1a. Throughout the storied history of Ohio State running backs, only two-time Heisman Trophy winner Archie Griffin has rushed for more yards.

Making Elliott's career accomplishments more impressive, he totaled his 3,961 rushing yards and 43 rushing touchdowns in Columbus in just three seasons.

The eventual No. 4 overall pick of the Dallas Cowboys, Elliott carried Ohio State to the 2015 College Football Playoff championship—almost literally. In three postseason games to close the 2014 campaign, Elliott totaled 696 yards and eight touchdowns, including 246 yards and four touchdowns in the national title game against Oregon.

Rushing for more than 1,800 yards in each of his two seasons as a starter from 2014 to '15, Elliott cemented his status as one of the best running backs ever to play at Ohio State—or anywhere else.

"He's one of the best players I've ever been around," Meyer said of Elliott in 2015.

Elliott's success, however, may not have been possible without the player he backed up during the Buckeyes' 2013 campaign, Carlos Hyde.

Prior to inheriting Hyde upon taking over the Ohio State program, Meyer had never had a running back rush for 1,000 yards in his offense. And although Hyde only managed to tally 970 yards in his first season under Meyer in 2012, he eventually crossed the 1,000-yard mark—and then some—with 1,521 yards in his senior season.

Thanks to Elliott and 2015 starter Mike Weber, a season hasn't passed since without a Buckeyes running back topping 1,000 yards.

Hyde, however, was the first and in the process laid the blueprint for power running backs to find success in Meyer's spread system. With

3,198 yards and 37 touchdowns to his credit, the 2014 second-round pick of the San Francisco 49ers will go down as one of the more underrated running backs in Ohio State history.

Second team: Brandon Warfield (Utah), Jeff Demps (Florida)
Honorable mention: Joe Alls (Bowling Green), Mike Weber (Ohio State), Marty Johnson (Utah), Deshawn Wynn (Florida)

H-Back: Percy Harvin

Also known as the pivot position, the "Percy Harvin position" in Urban Meyer's offense wouldn't be possible if not for, well, Percy Harvin.

Meyer had been using multiskilled players to diversify his offense and create mismatches for opposing defenses dating back to his days at Bowling Green. The pivot player is a wide receiver–running back hybrid who typically operates out of the slot.

"We put the APB out every year for the multidimensional athlete on offense," Meyer said in 2014. "Over the years, that position has evolved."

That evolution started with Harvin.

Lining up out wide, in the backfield, or in the slot while always maintaining the ability to shift in motion somewhere else, Harvin was a true nightmare for opponents throughout his three seasons in Gainesville. From 2006 to '08, the No. 2–ranked recruit in the 2006 class accumulated 3,781 yards and 32 total touchdowns. In each of his three seasons, the future Minnesota Vikings first-round pick tallied at least 400 rushing and 400 receiving yards, including 858 receiving and 764 rushing in 2007.

"I don't think I've ever been around a more dynamic athlete," Meyer said of Harvin.

Harvin wasn't the first to play his position in Meyer's offense, nor was he the last. Nobody, however, has played the "Percy Harvin position" better than Percy Harvin did.

Second team: Curtis Samuel (Ohio State)

Honorable mention: Paris Warren (Utah), Chris Rainey (Florida), Cole Magner (Bowling Green)

Wide Receivers: Devin Smith (Ohio State), Steve Savoy (Utah)

Given Meyer's propensity to play his best athletes at H-back, his wide receivers haven't produced the dominant numbers you'd necessarily expect from his explosive offenses.

The key for the wideouts in Meyer's spread system is to stretch the field. And none has done that better than Devin Smith.

In three seasons under Meyer, the speedster from Massillon, Ohio, proved to be one of the most dangerous deep threats in all of college football. From 2012 to '14, Smith tallied 107 catches for 2,209 yards and 26 touchdowns. Perhaps most impressively, in 2014 he averaged 28.2 yards per reception—a full four yards more than the next closest player in college football.

"We've done this for a long time. I want to say [he's] one of the best deep-ball players we've ever had," Meyer said of Smith in 2014.

At Utah, Steve Savoy filled a similar role.

In his two seasons playing under Meyer, Savoy totaled 107 catches for 1,624 yards and 18 touchdowns. In 2004, his 1,268 yards from scrimmage ranked No. 22 in the nation while his 961 receiving yards ranked No. 27. Without Savoy helping stretch the field for Alex Smith and Paris

Warren, it's hard to imagine the Utes successfully pulling off their run to an undefeated campaign.

Second team: Robert Redd (Bowling Green), Michael Thomas (Ohio State)

Honorable mention: Dallas Baker (Florida), Andre Caldwell (Florida), Corey "Philly" Brown (Ohio State), Riley Cooper (Florida)

Tight End: Aaron Hernandez

While there's no escaping the circumstances that brought his football career to an end, Aaron Hernandez's on-field accomplishments remain a part of Urban Meyer's history nonetheless.

In three seasons at Florida from 2007 to '09, Hernandez recorded 111 receptions for 1,382 yards and 12 touchdowns. Too big to be covered by a corner and too quick to match up with a safety, Hernandez was one of many mismatch problems for opposing defenses to deal with at Florida in the late 2000s. He won the 2009 John Mackey Award, which is presented the nation's top tight end, after tallying 68 catches for 850 yards and five touchdowns. That same season, he was named a first-team All-American.

In 2010, the New England Patriots selected Hernandez in the fourth round of the NFL draft. He went on to earn Pro Bowl alternate honors during the 2011 season.

In 2013, Hernandez was charged with first-degree murder following the killing of Odin Lloyd. A Massachusetts jury found him guilty of the charge. Hernandez died on April 19, 2017, from an apparent suicide while serving a sentence of life in prison without a possibility of parole.

Second team: Jeff Heuerman (Ohio State)

Honorable mention: Nick Vannett (Ohio State), Cornelius Ingram (Florida), Ben Moa (Utah)

Offensive Tackles: Taylor Decker (Ohio State), Jack Mewhort (Ohio State)

Since Meyer arrived at Ohio State in 2012, there's been one constant when it's come to the Buckeyes offensive line: the quarterback's blind side has been well protected.

"About important as it gets," Meyer said of the left tackle position in 2016.

It started in 2012, when the Buckeyes staff converted guard Jack Mewhort into their starting left tackle. For the next two seasons, the Toledo, Ohio, native served as the anchor of a unit that paved the way for the Ohio State offense to rank in the top 10 nationally in rushing both years.

In 2013, Mewhort earned All-American honors before being selected by the Indianapolis Colts in the second round of the NFL draft. That same season, Taylor Decker served as the Buckeyes' starting right tackle, before filling the void left by Mewhort on the left side of the line.

In his three seasons as a starter, Ohio State ranked in the top 11 in rushing nationally, while compiling a 38–4 record. In 2015, Decker followed in Mewhort's footsteps as an All-American, before the Detroit Lions made the 2015 Big Ten Offensive Lineman of the Year the first Buckeyes offensive lineman to be picked in the first round of the NFL draft since Nick Mangold in 2005.

Second team: Phil Trautwein (Florida), Marcus Gilbert (Florida)
Honorable mention: Tavo Tupola (Utah), Jamarco Jones (Ohio State)

Center: Maurkice Pouncey (Florida)

In his 15 years as a head coach, Meyer has started just two true freshmen on his offensive line. The first was Florida center Maurkice Pouncey.

A starter from the day his college career began in 2007, Pouncey went on to become one of the most decorated offensive linemen in SEC history. In 2009, the apex of the Gators offense earned consensus All-American honors, in addition to winning the Rimington Trophy, which is presented annually to the nation's top center.

The Pittsburgh Steelers selected Pouncey with the No. 18 overall pick in the 2010 NFL draft. He has since earned four trips to the Pro Bowl.

Second team: Mike Pouncey (Florida)
Honorable mention: Corey Linsley (Ohio State), Jesse Boone (Utah)

Guards: Pat Elflein (Ohio State), Chris Kemoeatu (Utah)

Prior to becoming Meyer's second Rimington Trophy winner as a center in 2016, Pat Elflein was already one of the best guards in college football. In both 2014 and 2015, Elflein was selected as a first-team All–Big Ten guard and in 2015, he was named a second-team All-American.

In addition to winning the Rimington, Elflein earned unanimous All-American honors in his senior season. The Minnesota Vikings selected the Pickerington, Ohio, native in the third round of the 2017 NFL draft.

A converted defensive lineman, Chris Kemoeatu became one of Meyer's most reliable offensive linemen throughout his two seasons at Utah. In 2004, Kemoeatu earned first-team All–Mountain West and All-American honors.

The Pittsburgh Steelers selected Kemoeatu in the sixth round of the 2005 draft. He went on to win two Super Bowls with the franchise.

Second team: Billy Price (Ohio State), Andrew Norwell (Ohio State)
Honorable mention: Dennis Wendel (Bowling Green)

Defensive Ends: Joey Bosa (Ohio State), Carlos Dunlap (Florida)

Of all the positions on the defensive side of the ball, none has wreaked more havoc for Meyer-coached teams than his defensive ends. And perhaps the best he's ever had when it comes to getting after quarterbacks was Joey Bosa, who was a standout player at Ohio State from the first day he set foot on the field.

Despite spending just three seasons in Columbus before entering the NFL draft, Bosa ended his career as the Buckeyes' third all-time sacks leader with 26. In 2014, he earned consensus All-American honors while helping lead Ohio State to the first-ever College Football Playoff championship.

Bosa was so impressive in his time with the Buckeyes that Meyer considered him to be not just the best defensive lineman he'd ever coached, but one of the best players, period. The San Diego Chargers picked Bosa with the No. 3 overall pick in the 2016 NFL draft, making him the highest-selected Ohio State player since the St. Louis Rams took Orlando Pace No. 1 overall in 1997.

Before he had Bosa on his side, Meyer benefitted at Florida from the play of star defensive end Carlos Dunlap. In three seasons with the Gators, Dunlap tallied 84 tackles, 26 of which came for a loss and 19.5 sacks. He was named the defensive MVP of the 2009 BCS National Championship Game a first-team All-SEC selection later that year.

The Cincinnati Bengals selected Dunlap in the second round of the 2010 NFL draft. In 2015, he made his first Pro Bowl with the team.

Second team: Derrick Harvey (Florida), John Simon (Ohio State)
Honorable mention: Jarvis Moss (Florida), Jermaine Cunningham (Florida), Tyquan Lewis (Ohio State), Alex Glantzis (Bowling Green), Sam Hubbard (Ohio State)

Defensive Tackles: Ray McDonald (Florida), Sione Po'uha (Utah)

Upon arriving in Gainesville, Meyer inherited one of the SEC's top defensive tackles in Ray McDonald. As a captain on Florida's 2006 national championship team, he tallied 36 tackles, 4.5 of which came for a loss, and three sacks, in addition to defending five passes and recovering one fumble for a touchdown. That same season, he earned first-team All-SEC honors.

The San Francisco 49ers selected McDonald in the third round of the 2007 NFL draft. He was go on to spend eight years in the league before legal troubles brought his football career to an end.

Recording 36 tackles, defending four passes, and tallying an interception, Sione Po'uha served as one of the standout defensive players on Utah's undefeated 2004 team. That same season, Po'uha was named a first-team All–Mountain West selection.

The New York Jets picked Po'uha in the third round of the 2005 NFL draft. He would go on to spend eight seasons with the franchise.

Second team: Adolphus Washington (Ohio State), Johnathan Hankins (Ohio State)

Honorable mention: Brandon Hicks (Bowling Green), Steve Fifita (Utah)

Outside Linebackers: Ryan Shazier (Ohio State), Darron Lee (Ohio State)

When Meyer first arrived at Ohio State, the cupboards were bare in the Buckeyes' linebackers room.

It didn't take long for that to change.

By the end of Meyer's second season in Columbus, the Ohio State staff had transformed Ryan Shazier into an All-America player. In his two seasons playing for Meyer, the future first-round pick of the Pittsburgh Steelers tallied 259 tackles, 40.5 of which came for a loss, and 12 sacks.

And yet even when Shazier headed off to the NFL, the Buckeyes didn't endure much of a drop-off, thanks to the development of a high school quarterback–turned–safety named Darron Lee. The third leading tackler and defensive Sugar Bowl MVP on Ohio State's 2014 national title team, Lee recorded 146 tackles, 27 of which came for a loss, and 11 sacks in his two seasons as a starter.

The New York Jets selected Lee with the No. 20 pick of the 2016 NFL draft.

Second team: Earl Everett (Florida), Joshua Perry (Ohio State)
Honorable mention: Ryan Stamper (Florida), Jerome Baker (Ohio State)

Middle Linebacker: Brandon Spikes (Florida)

While Tebow and Harvin served as the cornerstones of Meyer's highly touted 2006 recruiting class, it was linebacker Brandon Spikes who arrived in Gainesville as the class' biggest star on the defensive side of the ball.

The four-star prospect would prove to be worth the hype.

In four seasons with the Gators, Spikes won two national championships, recorded 307 tackles, 31.5 of which came for a loss, and 6.5 sacks, in addition to tallying six interceptions, four of which he returned for touchdowns. In both 2008 and 2009, he was named a consensus All-American.

The New England Patriots selected the three-time All-SEC selection in the second round of the 2010 NFL draft.

Second team: Raekwon McMillan (Ohio State)
Honorable mention: Brandon Siler (Florida), Zach Boren (Ohio State)

Cornerbacks: Joe Haden (Florida), Bradley Roby (Ohio State)

Much like his defensive lines, Meyer has found himself coaching a steady stream of future first-round picks in the back ends of his defense.

When it comes to lockdown corners, the best of the bunch has been Joe Haden, a converted high school quarterback who started as a true freshman at Florida in 2007. By the end of his final season with the Gators, Haden had won a national title, and been named a unanimous All-American and the *Sporting News* Defensive Player of the Year.

The Cleveland Browns selected Haden with the No. 7 overall pick in the 2007 draft and he has since earned two trips to the Pro Bowl.

Similarly, Bradley Roby parlayed his time with Meyer into a fruitful NFL future. After earning All-America honors in 2012 and twice being named a first-team All–Big Ten selection (2012, 2013), Roby was selected by the Denver Broncos in the first round of the 2014 NFL draft.

As a key piece on the Broncos defense, Roby helped Denver knock off the Carolina Panthers in Super Bowl 50.

Second team: Ryan Smith (Florida), Eli Apple (Ohio State)
Honorable mention: Janoris Jenkins (Florida), Janssen Patton (Bowling Green), Gareon Conley (Ohio State), Marshon Lattimore (Ohio State)

Safeties: Reggie Nelson (Florida), Malik Hooker (Ohio State)

After arriving in Gainesville as a junior-college transfer in Meyer's first season at Florida, safety Reggie Nelson quickly became one of the top players not only on the Gators defense, but in the entire nation.

In 2006, he tallied 51 tackles, five pass breakups, and six interceptions while leading Florida to the 2006 BCS national title. That same season, Nelson earned consensus All-America honors and won the Jack

Tatum Trophy, which is presented annually to the nation's top defensive back.

The Cincinnati Bengals selected Nelson with the No. 21 overall pick in the 2007 NFL draft. In 2015, he led the NFL in interceptions with eight.

Like Nelson, Malik Hooker's path to stardom was hardly a traditional one. The former three-star prospect arrived at Ohio State with little fanfare in the fall of 2014.

But by the end of his first season as a starter in 2016, Hooker had transformed into an instant star, earning unanimous All-American honors thanks to a regular season that saw him record 74 tackles, 5.5 of which came for a loss, and seven interceptions, three of which he returned for touchdowns, while leading the Buckeyes to the College Football Playoff.

Of all the defensive stars Meyer has coached, none has done more with the ball in his hands than Hooker did in 2016.

"I think every time I watch him, I'm going to flip him over on offense and pitch it to him a couple of times," Meyer said of Hooker's freakish athleticism. The Indianapolis Colts selected Hooker with the No. 15 overall pick in the 2017 NFL draft.

Second team: Vonn Bell (Ohio State), Eric Weddle (Utah)
Honorable mention: Ahmad Black (Florida), Morgan Scalley (Utah), Christian Bryant (Ohio State), Tyvis Powell (Ohio State)

Kicker: Shaun Suisham (Bowling Green)

Meyer would prefer not to need to rely on his kickers, but when he has had to, Bowling Green's Shaun Suisham was one of his most reliable. In 2002, Suisham connected on 12 of his 14 field-goal attempts for the Falcons and 57 of his 59 point-after attempts.

Suisham would go on to spend 10 years in the NFL from 2005 to '14, most notably with the Pittsburgh Steelers.

Second team: Jonathan Phillips (Florida)
Honorable mention: Chris Hetland (Florida)

Punter: Chas Henry (Florida)

If Meyer hates kicking, he despises punting. Luckily, when he did need to willingly give the ball back to his opponent at Florida, he typically had one of the nation's best in Chas Henry.

A four-year starter for the Gators, Henry averaged 43 yards per punt on 165 attempts throughout his college career. In 2010, after averaging 45.1 yards on 50 attempts, he was named a consensus All-American and the winner of the Ray Guy Award, which is presented to the nation's top punter.

He would go on to spend a season as the Philadelphia Eagles' starting punter in 2011.

Second team: Cameron Johnston (Ohio State)
Honorable mention: Eric Wilbur (Florida)

Return Specialist: Brandon James (Florida)

As a kick-return specialist, Brandon James twice earned All-America honors during his time in Gainesville.

In 2007, the Florida running back averaged 28 yards per kick return and 18.1 yards per punt return, including one touchdown score. The following year, he played a key part in the Gators' national-title run, returning two punts for touchdowns while averaging 13.8 yards per punt return and 23.1 yards per kick return. That season, he was also named the SEC's Special Teams Player of the Year.

Second team: Chris Rainey (Florida)
Honorable mention: Jalin Marshall (Ohio State)

★ ★ ★

What's Left?

On Thursday, August 31, 2017, the Ohio State football team will travel to Bloomington, Indiana, where Urban Meyer will kick off his sixth season as the Buckeyes' head coach.

By year's end, Meyer's tenure in Columbus will have matched his six seasons in Gainesville for the longest stint of his coaching career.

Back when Meyer accepted the Ohio State head coaching job in late 2011, not many viewed it as a long-term match. Perhaps it was because of the previously nomadic nature of his coaching career, in which prior to his six years at Florida, he had only held two jobs over the course of 18 years for longer than two years. But the biggest reason why many have often considered the now-52-year-old Meyer as a candidate for early retirement is the abrupt way in which he left Florida and a fear that a similar departure from Ohio State could be ahead.

Yet as Meyer prepares to begin his sixth season as the head coach of the Buckeyes, he clearly appears to be in a different place than he was eight years ago.

He's healthier. He's more easygoing with the press. Even at what appears to be a crossroads of sorts for Ohio State under his watch, Meyer appears better equipped to handle the shortcomings of his program and the inevitable transition that's become a reality of today's modern age of college football.

Make no mistake; even with his 61–6 record over the course of the previous five seasons, two College Football Playoff appearances, and one national championship, the Buckeyes program is far from perfect. Ohio State's offense is in the midst of an overhaul after underperforming for the better part of the previous two seasons, and the Buckeyes face threats across the country in not only the powerhouse that is Alabama, but rising programs at Clemson and Michigan.

But under Meyer's watch, the Ohio State program remains as healthy as it's ever been. On National Signing Day 2017, the Buckeyes added another top-five class—Meyer's fifth in six signing days at the helm of Ohio State.

"For me that left this facility very quickly," Meyer said of the Buckeyes' Fiesta Bowl loss to the Tigers. "We delved into recruiting, finished off one of the best classes in history, and the team is at it and going at it with the intent that that will never happen again."

Unlike when he left Florida, Meyer's success with the Buckeyes appears set up for the long haul.

Of course, it remains possible that Meyer could once abruptly leave, perhaps riding off into the sunset on his own terms. After all, nobody in Gainesville foresaw the sudden way in which his time at Florida came to an end.

But as long as Meyer is still on Ohio State's sideline, the Buckeyes will remain one of the premier programs in college football. And in the process, Meyer will continue to add to his historic coaching résumé.

With his career still in process, Meyer has already made as strong of a case as any for being considered the sport's best.

From the numbers to the journey, it's a legacy unlike any other in college football history.

★ ★ ★

Sources

The author would like to acknowledge the reporters and columnists who have covered Urban Meyer and the various coaches discussed in this book.

In many instances, the author used quotes obtained from postgame press conferences and various media gatherings. He may have also repurposed quotes and information from his previous work at Rivals.com, Buckeye Sports Bulletin, Bleacher Report, and Land of 10.

Other quotes and information came from various sources. Those sources include the following:

Websites

AlligatorSports.org
BuckeyeSports.com
ElevenWarriors.com
ESPN.com
FoxSports.com
MaxPreps.com
MGoBlue.com
Sports-Reference.com
TheOzone.net
TulsaWorld.com

News Organizations

South Florida Sun Sentinel

New York Times

Associated Press

Daily Iowan

Greenville News

New York *Daily News*

Los Angeles Times

Orlando Sentinel

Sporting News

Michigan Daily

Cleveland Plain Dealer

Atlanta Journal-Constitution

Raleigh Register

Cincinnati Enquirer

Books

Martin, Buddy. *Urban's Way: Urban Meyer, the Florida Gators, and His Plan to Win.* New York: St. Martin's Griffin, 2009.

Schembechler, Bo, and Mitch Albom. *Bo: Life, Laughs, and Lessons of a College Football Legend.* New York: Warner Books, 1989.

Schlabach, Mark. *Called to Coach: Reflections on Life, Faith, and Football.* Brentwood, Tennessee: Howard Books, 2011.

Chastian, Bill. *The Steve Spurrier Story: From Heisman to Head Ball Coach.* Lanham, Maryland: Taylor Trade Publishing, 2002.

Other Media

Fox Sports' "The Herd"